Through a Glass Darkly

The Ambiguity
of the Christian Tradition

Donald L. Berry

UNIVERSITY PRESS OF AMERICA,® INC.

Lanham • *Boulder* • *New York* • *Toronto* • *Oxford*

Copyright © 2006 by
University Press of America,® Inc.
4501 Forbes Boulevard
Suite 200
Lanham, Maryland 20706
UPA Acquisitions Department (301) 459-3366

PO Box 317
Oxford
OX2 9RU, UK

Library of Congress Control Number: 2006929292
ISBN-13: 978-0-7618-3547-9 (paperback : alk. paper)
ISBN-10: 0-7618-3547-4 (paperback : alk. paper)

FOR

Wanda, Martha, and Ruth
Samuel and Benjamin
Unfailing bearers of light

"For now we see through a glass, darkly,
but then, face to face. Now I know in part;
but then shall I know even as also I am known."

I Corinthians 13:12 [KJV]

Contents

Preface

I have, for some time, been distressed by the religious passion and the political power demonstrated by many persons and groups who, despite their important differences, seek to impose on the general population ethical views which they claim to be derived from the Bible, and which accordingly are held to have prescriptive value for all persons, without respect to their possibly very different religious commitments. The religious pluralism of American society and the separation of church and state affirmed in the Federal Constitution appear to be irrelevant to those who want to impose "God's law" on the land as a whole. They speak and act as if [1] the meaning of biblical texts is self-evident, not admitting of divergent interpretation; [2] that it is possible to derive a clear, consistent, and detailed ethical mandate from the Bible; [3] that the Bible and the God to whom it refers have defined how all persons should live, whether they believe in this God or acknowledge the Bible's presumed authority. I reject each of these claims, and do so in the name of a religiousness that eschews the need for absolutes, and which seeks always to be informed both by the best scientific knowledge about the nature and development of life on earth, and also by the best available historical-critical understanding of the Christian tradition—its origin and continuing life, basic texts, central affirmations, and life-policy proposals. When one examines the tradition in the light of this information, one is impressed by the way various kinds of ambiguity are attached to every major component of the tradition. An acceptance of that characteristic must become a determining factor in the way Christian faith is articulated and defended, and the way its political interests are expressed. For the churches and for those who speak for them not to do so would be dishonest, and the consequent obscurantism would make Christian belief even harder for an intelligent person to adopt and to defend in a religiously pluralistic environment.

In this book I seek to explore the way ambiguity emerges as an important ingredient in the Christian paradigm, and how an appropriation of this feature can make the Christian voice less demanding and more inviting, less strident and more healing. My aim here is to examine the ways in which four elements of the tradition might appear if examined through the truth-disclosing lens of ambiguity. The chapters progress from the most general to the most specific. In Chapter One—"The Story"—I give a narrative reading of the Christian reality with as little use as possible of the inherited technical theological language. This should allow the bright and dark sides of the Christian story to be recognized by any open-minded person who may or may not have explicit ecclesiastical loyalties. Chapter Two—"The Book"—investigates how one might properly allocate authority to the biblical texts without regarding them as inerrant or infallibly true, that is, in the light of certain necessary constraints, how and what one can mean when speaking of the Bible as the Word of God. In Chapter Three—"The Man"—I explain how the tradition's more technical language about the life and work of Jesus of Nazareth [its Christology] might be revitalized if one were to find a way of living with the ambiguity involved in naming Jesus as the Christ, or as the Son of God. In Chapter Four— "The Friend"—I narrow the focus, looking at a single feature in the life of Jesus, the way his self-understanding, at least as this is represented in the gospel narratives, facilitated intimate friendship relations with two persons—Mary of Magdala, and John the son of Zebedee. My aim here is to suggest how the ambiguous nature of Jesus' humanity points us to a fresh, life-enhancing picture of friendship. Just as the Bible continues to inspire us because of, not despite, it ambiguity, so the historical Jesus continues to model the potential of life for us because of, not despite, its ambiguity.

An early version of the material presented in Chapter One was given as a lecture in the Colgate University series on the Great Religions of the World, on March 7, 1991. Its title then was "The Humanity of God: A Reading of the Christian Tradition." Some material in Chapter Two is a revision of an article that appeared as "The Bible as an Earthen Vessel: A Plea for Biblical Honesty," in *Encounter* [Vol. 58:4, Autumn 1997], pp. 413-418. Chapter Three was originally published as "Revisioning Christology: The Logic of Messianic Ascription," in *The Anglican Theological Review*, [Vol. LXX:2, April 1988], pp. 129-140. I gratefully acknowledge permission to reprint these materials here, with extensive revisions.

Many of the ideas in this book were shared and developed over the years with members of The Conference of Anglican Theologians, colleagues in the Colgate University Department of Philosophy and Religion, and students in my classes, who, in their perceptive responses, confirmed for me the necessity and value of asking "But what does that mean?" Support for manuscript preparation and conference participation was generously provided by Colgate University through funds attached to the Harry Emerson Fosdick Chair in Philosophy and Religion, to which I was appointed in 1989. I am very appreciative of this important assistance.

Wanda Warren Berry, my wife and colleague, has facilitated this project in many ways, not the least of which has been her partnership in a continuing dialogue through which the significance of these matters, about which both of us care very deeply, has always been understood. This book is dedicated to her, and to our daughters, Martha and Ruth who invest our life with grace and joy beyond measure, and to our grandsons, Samuel and Benjamin, unfailing bearers of light.

Chapter One

The Story

Neither the critics nor the defenders of the Christian tradition have paid sufficient attention to its ambiguity. Some critics have so emphasized the tradition's undoubted complicity in oppression of many kinds that one might reasonably wonder what life-enhancing dynamic could ever have been so powerful as to attract thoughtful women and men to this society. Some defenders have so emphasized the transforming power of the grace the community undoubtedly transmits that one might reasonably wonder what would lead thoughtful men and women to regard the support of slavery, the marginalization of women, and the maltreatment of gay and lesbian brothers and sisters as minor deviations and temporary aberrations of the gospel call to human liberation. What we need is a healthy and honest appreciation of the tradition's inherent ambiguity. Accordingly, I want to identify a central, defining aspect of the Christian life—its origin, significance, and how it might account for the continuing vitality of this tradition despite the misunderstandings, the massive distortions, and the dark complicity in oppression that also have characterized so much of its institutional life. I will suggest the dynamic which helps to illuminate the remarkable diversity and tension among the several ways in which Christian women and men have sought to express themselves religiously. Although no attempt is made here to describe and evaluate the range of Christian creedal affirmation, liturgical expression, ethical recommendation, and ecclesiastical formation, the praxis of the two major Christian variations should be discernible: the Catholic variation [Roman, Anglican, and Orthodox], the Protestant variation [both magisterial and free forms].

Insofar as possible, I will quite deliberately avoid using the inherited theological vocabulary. I will do this for two reasons. First, articulators of the tradition have usually attempted to explicate a theological statement by employing additional theological terms. But the meaning of the language of faith is not self-evident, and cannot be clarified simply by repetition or by the expansion of the theological vocabulary. The critic and the believer alike are entitled to ask "Just what does this creed mean?" That question requires an answer phrased in the most accessible manner possible. The question of Christian meaning cannot be kept an intramural matter.

Second, critics and defenders of the tradition alike fail to take seriously the metaphorical and adjectival nature of religious and theological language. The language of belief is the product of human creativity and imagination, and is thus always secondary to the transforming and illuminating event. First the encounter, then the dance, and only then the story.

1. THE BRIGHT STORY BEGINS[1]

The Christian form of life began as a movement for renewal and reform within Palestinian Jewish society in the first century of the Common Era. It was one of several ways in which Jewish women and men sought to improve the conditions of their life, deepen its meaning, and expand the possibilities of its significance. This movement was inaugurated by the activity of an itinerant Jewish teacher named Jesus, from the village of Nazareth in the northern, ethnically diverse district of the Galilee. He talked about the grandeur of lilies, and the peril of self-obsession; he celebrated the largess of vicarious love, and denounced the structures and agents of exploitation; he insisted that the motive of our acting was as subject to ethical scrutiny as the detail of our action; he cherished his solitude and enjoyed parties, disregarding the dominant conventions governing the candidates and conditions for social behavior. He commended and embodied a style of living in which concern for the degraded and ignored, and solidarity with those on the margins is the imperative to follow at whatever cost to oneself. He shared this vision with others in talk, observation, in commentary, dialogue, and supportive action—illuminating the minds of women and men, invigorating their wills, and challenging their loves. Many of those who met him were surprised by his extraordinary inclusion, had a sense of being released from destructive bondages, and found their lives being changed for the better.

He was accompanied on his walking tours by a group of men and women, the most prominent being Simon [nicknamed "Peter" or "Rocky"], Mary [from the Galilean lake-shore village of Magdala], and the brothers James and John, with the latter of whom, together with Mary, Jesus seems to have been especially close. His work was financially underwritten by several women of substantial means, and his activity was regarded with enthusiasm by some people and as a threat by others, especially those who had an interest in preserving the status quo. After a short public career of several months, he took his program to Jerusalem, his nation's capital, where both the adulation and the opposition became intense, and where, within a few days he was executed as being politically dangerous by the Roman occupation authority. On the night before his execution, he shared a farewell meal with the inner circle of his friends. During supper he identified the broken bread and out-poured wine of that meal with his own life situation, anticipating that his vocational fidelity would soon lead to his death. He enjoined his friends to remember that, and thus to remember him, whenever they ate and drank together again.

A few days after his death, two of his friends reported an unusual happening.[2] They had invited a strange but interesting conversation partner to have supper with them one night at their house in a village nearby to Jerusalem. During the course of their meal, the stranger seemed to move from being guest to being himself the host, and in the breaking of the bread Jesus' friends recognized their guest to be Jesus himself. About the same time, others of his friends, joined now by his mother, Mary, and his brothers, began to meet together in a private home in Jerusalem. In the course of their being with one another, they came finally to understand that a life policy of caring is what human life is all about. They, too, began to have a vivid sense of Jesus' continuing presence among them. Empowered by that conviction and sense of remarkable presence, they began to tell the Jesus story to others, and to recommend this vision of life's possibility to them. They gathered regularly to talk, to read and reflect, to pray and sing, and always to share the bread and wine "for the remembrance" of him. This kept them in touch with the one who shows what being a neighbor to the other was like, and whose continuing presence released them from self-occupation so that they could become just such a companion to another.

Within a few years there were similar assemblies in many of the urban, Greek-speaking centers of the Mediterranean basin. The dynamic of this Jesus movement had burst the boundaries of its Palestinian and Jewish origins, and had become a transracial and transnational network of communities. A gender-neutral ritual lustration, baptism, had replaced circumcision as the badge of belonging, and the first day had replaced the seventh as the day on which the people celebrated his presence, and were nourished with the empowering bread and wine. They began soon to speak of that blessed and shared bread and wine under the metaphor of the body and blood of their friend who, although dead, still inhabited their midst. From almost the beginning, these Jesus societies rejected the relevance of the sexual, racial, and economic distinctions common to the Roman world. They organized themselves as communities of equals. Being male or female, Jew or Gentile, slave or free was neither a barrier nor an entitlement. Women and men alike presided over their gatherings and liturgies; they were partners in searching for the most appropriate language to express their new identity; and they were joint architects and agents of their program of witness and hospitality.

In this first generation, Jesus-the-messenger became Jesus-the-message, and the house assemblies began to employ increasingly extravagant metaphors and honorifics to symbolize the value he had come to have for them, and to elucidate the meaning for their lives of his continuing accessibility. But those who followed this new way never regarded themselves as a memorial society, meeting simply to remember a dead hero or to pay regular respects to a departed leader.

After a little more than a hundred years, these moral hospitals and colonies of loyalty had developed relatively fixed patterns of speaking, behavior, and organization that seemed to them to be ways of making explicit the nature of the originative event, and to provide its power for successive generations. These patterns consisted, in part, of summary statements of belief, an anthology of narratives and letters to be read and commented upon, a symbolic meal, and a three-fold structure of leadership: bishops, priests, and deacons. These patterns provided the parameters by and within which women and men were able, in diverse ways, to live out the alternative life option associated with Jesus of Nazareth. The umbrella, collective name they chose for these normative patterns, forms, and structures was "church." This "church" was for them the communal extension in continuing time and space of the good news Jesus announced, commenced, and embodied. It is as if the body who instructed veteran fishermen about how to fish and who embraced Mary and John, had become the body they shared at table, and now had become the body who embraced them all. They tell us that being part of this body was like being in a new family, receiving a new identity. They felt themselves freed from the determining power of the past, rescued from the lie of aloneness, and opened to the future with diminished fear. That was good news indeed!

2. THE DARK SIDE

But there was bad news as well, and it was not long in coming. Four shifts in attitude, consciousness, and social arrangement took place between the second and fourth centuries, whose consequence significantly altered the Christian posture in the world, and bequeathed a dark and heavy legacy of confusion. We have yet to extricate ourselves from this malaise, although countervailing forces do appear to be moderately effective here and there, and from time to time.

[1] The first distortion concerns the nature of power, and can best be described as the shift from a horizontal to a vertical understanding and operation of power relationships within the several church communities. What began as a functional distinction became by the second century a metaphysical one. A variety of functions was discovered to be necessary for their common life: presiding at gatherings for worship and the sacred meal, teaching and explaining the content of believing, caring for the physical needs of one another, working out the ethical corollary of faith, and the like. All tasks were important for upbuilding the life of the conventicles of the Way. Since all were authorized by the same Spirit, the performance of no one of them conferred status superior to the others. But a concern for protection in a hostile environment, and a need to provide for continuity of identity in an uncertain world soon changed power sharing for mutual service, into power hierarchically structured. Obedience displaced consultation; holding an office displaced simply doing what needed to be done. It was not so at the beginning. And voices from that more egalitarian vision continued to insist on another way, sometimes impatiently and often with penalty. We are now only beginning to recover the appropriateness of a model of power that rejects a hierarchy of privilege and seeks a model of power sharing that takes with utmost seriousness the new identity conferred upon all persons in the body by virtue of their membership

[2] The second distortion is an aspect of the first, and concerns the tragic betrayal of women. In the beginning women shared with men all the functions of the new communities — sponsoring, educating, presiding. The equality that characterized the early colonies of faith was expressed not only in the way power was structured, but also in the identity of the power sharers. The egalitarian authority structure was accompanied by an egalitarian sexual agenda, limited, to be sure, by the heterosexist paradigm of ancient consciousness. But by the middle of the second century, the churches[3] had succumbed to the patriarchal ethos of the Mediterranean world, and women came more and more to occupy a derivative, subordinate, and adjunct status. This could be sanctioned only by reading the texts, which had come to be authoritative, through a patriarchal lens that was as pejorative, as selective, and as distorting then as it is now. Although the more woman-affirming strata of those texts could not be expunged,[4] they were overlaid by androcentric instructions. Thus, the marginalization of women became the despair, the malodorous sickness from which the church as a whole has not yet recovered. It is a matter of great irony that this misogynist policy was accompanied by a dramatically increased attention to the figure of Mary, the mother of Jesus. Such a

development was possible only by fashioning Mary's story and devotion in such a way as to picture her as essentially sexless, a non-threatening model defined by celibate males. This constraint on the well-being of the community is indicted and given the charter for its correction by the same factor that will move the churches to correct their dominant power model. This factor is baptism, the gender-neutral, gender-inclusive act of incorporation, which patriarchy has never understood, but which patriarchy has never been able to ignore or wholly to assimilate to its own demonic interests.

[3] The third distortion is closely connected to the second, and concerns the invasion of Christian consciousness, in the second to the fourth centuries, by anti-body, anti-material, and anti-sexual modes of thought. All renovating religious systems assume that there is something amiss with respect to the given life situation of women and men, and such systems can be distinguished from one another by the resolution they propose for such mis-focused existence. The Jesus movement shares with its rabbinic sibling the conviction that this quotidian, material, bodily, and sexual realm is an appropriate context in which women and men may live a meaningful life. The Christian emphasis on how this follows from the life of Jesus as a fully historical, fully human person, that means fully sexual, being is a special focus of the inherited Jewish affirmation of the essential value of the material world. That affirmation is epitomized in the familiar line from one of ancient Israel's poets: "and God saw everything that he had made, and behold it was very good." [Genesis 1:31] The human predicament, in such a view, is not occasioned by our living amidst material things and beings, but by our loving those things and beings in a possessive way. This perspective was suppressed, however, as the churches' intellectual leaders sought to explicate the Christian vision in a way that would make believable contact with the dominant conceptual categories of the sophisticated Roman world. In that venture they appropriated the Neo-Platonic vision which assumed that the material world was in itself the barrier to a richly lived life. They did not recognize the inner contradiction of such attention to the finite, nor did they see that in making such a move, they had not really escaped the gnostic hatred of the body. The consequence of this misadventure was twofold: a preference for an otherworldly realm, and a preference for virginity and celibacy as primary virtues. Augustine's phallic fixation twisted the tradition's ethical focus for a thousand years, and was not really corrected by the revival with Aquinas of the Aristotelian acceptance of the material world, since Aquinas insisted upon the incompleteness of that very world, and built on Aristotle's deficient view of human nature. We have yet to overcome this baleful legacy, but whenever someone understands the implications of sharing broken bread and outpoured wine, she or he finds permission for seeing the "celebration of flesh" and bodily embrace as signs of the deepest realities of human life.[5]

[4] The fourth distortion concerns the relation of church and society, and can be described as the shift away from the principle of voluntary association and a network of witnesses to an alliance with the state and dependence on the rewards of juridical endorsement. Faith communities were, by the beginning of the fourth century, well rooted in almost all of the major urban centers of the Roman Empire, leading a valiant, productive, and, for the most part, a peaceful if legally precarious existence. The genius of Constantine ended the churches' ambiguous situation, and in his century the increasingly centralized church moved from being unrecognized to being legally tolerated, then state supported, and finally to being the only licit religious institution in the Roman world. With the transfer to it of the basilicas, temples, and other properties of the old religions, something called "Christendom" was born. Satisfaction with privilege and advantage replaced contentment with argument, example, and story-telling. In this misalliance the church's existence was secured, to be sure, but at the cost of a severe modulation of its critical, prophetic voice.

The catalogue of consequences is long and well-known. I name here only a few: oppression of all kinds of minorities—religious, ethnic, sexual; superficial commitment and inexpensive grace; the folly of the Crusades, the grotesquery of the Inquisition, the shame of colonization, acquiescence in genocide and slavery, and the spoilation of indigenous cultures—all manifestations of destructive triumphalism. Although "Christendom," for the most part, has been disestablished both legally and culturally, its memory as a vanished ideal still haunts many of our contemporaries. In a self-serving way, some bishops, commercial evangelists, and their legislative and judicial allies seek to use the agencies and instrumentalities of the state to impose restrictive views of particular communities on the general population. The credibility of religious faith can only be diminished by such efforts.

3. THE BRIGHT SIDE PERSISTS

These shifts are quite properly designated "distortions" and "betrayals" of the originating insight and early Christian praxis. Nothing that follows should in any way be regarded as gainsaying the perfidy and human cost of these transformations. Nonetheless, there were gains and goods as well that came about, despite the obstacles that have been identified here. From this other part of the story we should note the following as examples of the ability of the authentic vision to emerge or to be conveyed even by defective instruments.

[1] Structures have been devised and staffed, from hospice and hospital to kitchen, food cupboard, and sanctuary to care for the wounded, the hungry, and the displaced.

[2] In the pre-nuclear age when war was more thinkable as an instrument of national policy, procedures were devised to lessen the brutal inhumanity of military conflict. The theory exemplified by these rules was given the name "just war," an oxymoron in a more perfect world.

[3] Music, painting, sculpture, and the other arts were sponsored and encouraged as appropriate expressions of human creativity and of the view that the material world can be the venue of significant meaning.

[4] Religious orders and houses provided for the education and leadership of both women and men, and rescued much of the literary heritage of the ancient world from destruction.

[5] Systems of thought were developed in which persons sought to synthesize key concerns of religious faith and dominant assumptions about the nature of reality. The categories of Plato, Aristotle, the Romantics, Kierkegaard, James, Dewey, Freud, Jung, and Marx, among others, have been utilized to suggest the reasonableness of believing.

[6] The transnational character of the Christian movement served, for a time, to soften the excesses of nationalist aspiration and to point to a common and higher loyalty. Such an appeal was not wholly lost even with the sad, eleventh century separation of the Eastern from the Latin Church, or the unhappy rupture of the latter in the sixteenth century events of Reformation and Counter-Reformation.

[7] Poets, critics, and mystics who gave voice to the more fundamental vision were tolerated, never fully silenced, and were occasionally heard and heeded.

That the Christian story came to have both dark and bright sides should be no surprise to anyone who appreciates both the dynamic of the faith image of Jesus and the limited possibilities for justice in an imperfect world. In what the tradition will call "a fallen world," moral possibilities decrease as the complexity of the society increases. Two features of this story bear further comment if we are fully to understand the dynamics of this dark and bright tradition.

First, there is no contradiction between affirming both the normative character of the first century experience for the subsequent tradition, and the necessity of development and reformulation. The Catholic communities, more in the West than in the East, have always regarded historical development as not only a fact of institutional life, but also as the way in which the church comes to a clearer understanding of the originary event. Protestants have tended to be more suspicious of development, and have given the first Christian century a more mythical and determinative status. But development and change there would be as the audience of the story itself changes and grows. The only problem development as such creates for the tradition is a formal one—the need to identify the criteria by which appropriate life-giving movement can be distinguished from cancerous growth. Men and women of goodwill can and do disagree on the context and application of these criteria. That fact accounts in part for the continuing pluralism of the Christian tradition.

Second, since this faith perspective seeks the renovation of human life in all its dimensions, the church communities must be politically involved if the economic and social structures that hold men and women in thrall are to be altered, as altered they must be if liberation is ever to become even a proximate reality. Politics is an immediate implication of religious faith, but women and men of goodwill can and do disagree on the mode of involvement that will ensure the independence of the church, the effectiveness of ethical action, and the inviolability of the rights of all persons. This fact helps to account for the continuing tension among and within the several Christian communions.

Development and involvement over the centuries have caused both the bright and dark sides to appear. Another way to put this is to observe that despite massive deformations, the power of the initial paradigm is still present. What remains now to do is to suggest briefly just how such vitality in the midst of sickness is best understood.

4. THE STORY CONTINUES

The Christian shares with all other religious traditions this tension between a life-enhancing impetus and life-limiting developments. Furthermore, the church is no different, formally speaking, from all other institutions. An initial experience receives a social expression that changes and develops over the years, and in the course of its life the institution acts in ways that seem to contradict the original vision. The creative insight then tends to surface again in different ways to remind, recall, and to reform the society. If the society persists in time, this process becomes a dialectical one.

Consider the American democratic state, born in a revolution for liberty that nonetheless tolerated and profited from slavery, the most nefarious of economic arrangements, and expanded from the Atlantic to the Pacific by genocide of the native populations. But the corruption of the ideal of freedom remains a corrigible problem; and from time to time discerning voices call us back to our defining possibility, not by appealing to some new alien program, but by pursuing the primary idea with new insights. Lincoln's "Gettysburg Address," Dr. King's "I Have a Dream" speech, or his "Letter from Birmingham Jail" are cases in point. In a related context, one should add to such a brief list Susan B. Anthony's voting in the 1872 presidential election in

Rochester, New York, fifty-two years before the Nineteenth Amendment was ratified—an action surely consistent with the deepest meaning of the country's founding documents. We have yet to act as if we fully understood Jefferson's words to be an invitation to us to "hold these truths to be self-evident, that all [women and] men are created equal."

Consider the church in an analogous way, and we should be prepared to acknowledge the bright and dark sides of its history, the calls for reformation and depth-renewal, and the capacity for self-correction. The dynamic of the church's life is thus quite similar to that of other institutions. One characteristic, however, seems to distinguish the church from other societies, and this is the nature of its self-corrective power. In those moments when it is true to itself, the community knows itself as a pilgrim people, always on-the-way; not a group of moral athletes who have it made, but a gathering of wounded and wounding women and men who admit this about themselves, and who are never more than in the process of becoming whole care-givers. These women and men do not persist by appealing to an ideal, however lofty, or to a principle, however cogent; nor do they count simply on good will, rationality, or common history. Rather, they find themselves empowered by their identification with the Man from Nazareth in his *disponibilite*, his life broken open and poured out for others.

Such a form of life requires a symbolic consciousness, an openness to the power of metaphor, and an appreciation of gesture—both to stimulate and to feed the imagination. From such a perspective Christian women and men have discerned the capacity of song and sermon, of dance and deed, of institutional office and intellectual endeavor authentically to convey life-giving power. This empowerment makes a responsible present possible because the determining hold of the past has been nullified, and the future has been genuinely opened. But the bread and wine of this new humanity are contained in earthen vessels, allowing no self-congratulation, but eliciting gratitude and radical astonishment. The chalice is thus the sign and the agency of the Christian life wherever it is lived most fully and with appropriate humility.

NOTES

1. Almost every sentence in this chapter contains a judgment or interpreting decisions with respect to the sources available to us. My aim is to convey those conclusions in a non-technical manner, but I do not here discuss the evidence or rehearse the options that critical analysis permits.

2 This is, of course, a reference to the Walk to Emmaus pericope [Luke 24:13–35]. Although I include that episode here in this narrative of Christian beginnings, I am

not claiming it to be an authentic historical event as such, at least not in its present form. Its congruence with the genre of an appearance narrative [{i} the risen Jesus encounters some person[s]; {ii} he is not recognized; {iii} he acts or speaks in such a way as to disclose his identity; {iv} he is finally recognized], and the presence of the churches' eucharistic language ["the breaking of the bread"], suggests that the evangelist at this point has given narrative expression to certain features of the community's liturgical experience. My purpose in including reference to this pericope now is simply to call attention to the location of the eucharist in the earliest life of the Christian assemblies, a characteristic which I do regard as fully historical.

3. I use the plural form "churches" to refer to the networks of Christian assemblies that were beginning to take shape in this early period. Using the singular form "church" to refer to the Christian reality in the pre-Constantinian era would suggest a degree of uniformity and collective formation for which there is no historical evidence.

4. As I will point out in the discussion in the next chapter of the self-corrective dynamic of the canonical process, an anti-female tendency is discernible at an early point in the history of the Western Text tradition.

5. I have discussed this issue further in "Seeking a Theology of the Finite," *The Christian Century*, Vol. 99, No. 29 [September 29, 1982], pp. 953–956; see also "The Body and the Polis," in my *An Inquiry into the Nature and Usefulness of a Perspectival Approach to the Study of Religion* [Lewiston: The Edwin Mellen Press, 1991], pp. 95–126.

Chapter Two

The Book

In the previous chapter I observed how the Christian tradition has both a bright and a dark side. Recognition of such ambiguity is important if the tradition is to speak with any life-enhancing power to persons possessed of a modern sensibility. That power is diminished for those defenders of the tradition who fail to recognize its complicity in the many forms of human oppression, or who regard the Christian aegis of racist, sexist, and homophobic actions as but minor and temporary aberrations. That power is obscured for those critics of the tradition who regard its betrayals as definitive evidence of its true character. Neither defender nor critic properly appreciates the necessary fallibility, that is to say, the ambiguity of institutional embodiments of religious vision.

The feature of the tradition that exposes in a clear way the possibility and peril of the tradition is the status which is accorded the Bible. What I seek to do in this chapter is to indicate how much discussion of the so-called authority[1] of the Bible rests upon a category mistake, and how an awareness of this hermeneutical error can lead to an increase of intellectual honesty and religious effectiveness.[2]

1. BIBLICAL AUTHORITY AS A PROBLEM

Every candidate for ordination to the priesthood in the Episcopal Church is required to declare that he or she believes ". . . the Holy Scriptures of the Old and New Testaments to be the Word of God, and to contain all things necessary for salvation."[3] That the "Old" and "New" Testaments[4] function authoritatively for individuals and societies in the Christian tradition is evidenced in

many different ways: biblical texts are regarded as the basis of doctrinal formulations, a source of historical information, a foundation for ethical pre-
scriptions and evangelistic programs, as well as furnishing phrases and words
that are employed less systematically in various formal and informal linguistic contexts. But of particular interest here is the widespread use of the "Word
of God" metaphor to justify this ascription of authority. Such usage is most
often uncritical, that is, without an appeal to any particular theory or explanatory framework. The absence of careful attention to the several meanings that regarding something as "authoritative" can have makes it very difficult to know what is being claimed in speaking of the Bible as the "Word of
God," since, whatever else may be intended, all use of "Word of God" with
reference to the Bible is a way of saying that the biblical writings are authoritative in some sense. The situation is complicated further by the need to distinguish between saying that the Bible "*is* the Word of God," and speaking of
the Bible "*as* the Word of God." The latter phrase is an explicit recognition of
the metaphorical status of "Word of God," but the metaphorical status of the
former phrase is scarcely less disguised, even if not always recognized.

All theological language is the product of the creative human imagination,[5]
but much of the fundamentalist discourse about biblical authority which employs "the Bible is the Word of God" conceptuality fails to recognize this, and
is thus unable fully to appreciate the relativity and historically conditioned
character of all theological language. Consider, for example, three statements
that are representative of this perspective.

[1] In defiance of well-known historical fact, Stephen F. Nall claims, "The
literalness of Scripture has been the church's foundation of self-identity from
apostolic times, a defense against the fantasies of heretics."[6] Nall seems to
forget that the canon was a second century idea, and that its present form was
fixed only in 367 AD, and then by Athanasius' Festal Letter, not by conciliar
action. The self-identity of the dominant ecclesial community was in the
process of being shaped in relation to the development of creed, episcopate,
and canon, all of which were post-apostolic achievements, although they have
apostolic roots. This development took place in the period in which Christian
assemblies were following various routes to self-identity. The diversity of
Christian institutional formation in the pre-Constantinian era is reflected in
the diversity of Christian attitudes toward both the appropriate content and
meaning of the Bible. Nall forgets that early Christian commentators did not
understand themselves to be obligated to attend naively to the "literalness of
the text." They recognized the polysemous character of biblical writing, and
developed a variety of hermeneutical strategies [e.g., allegorical, typological]
to deal with its often puzzling style and self-contradictory accounts. Clement
of Alexandria's [c. 156–215 AD] assessment of the Fourth Gospel as a "spir-

itual" gospel[7] is evidence of a very early awareness that an appeal to the "literalness of the text" is an inadequate principle of biblical interpretation. It is not at all clear what one could intelligibly mean by speaking of "the literalness of Scripture," given the great variety of poetic and other genres used by the biblical authors

[2] Ted Nelson seems to be aware that biblical texts do contain symbols, although he seeks to grant them an inappropriate status: "Pray that in our worship we will continue to hold fast to the language and symbols through which God has revealed Himself."[8] Since we have considerable information about the writing and composition of the documents included in the several Jewish and Christian canons, it simply is not clear what it could mean to say of them that the symbols and metaphors are the product of God's self-revelation. In his rejection of the appropriateness of inclusive language, Nelson is apparently claiming that the biblical language itself is divinely authored. Such a view, however forgets that all the biblical texts, as well as all the doctrinal formulations of the churches, are historically conditioned human documents. Their ability to be disclosive of salvific power does not depend on their being literally true. To regard them as revelatory of God, that is, to regard them as having authority, cannot mean that they are infallible, only that they are light-giving and meaning-conveying. Although the authors may be said to be inspired, their work can only be inspiring. That means that the reader's situation and response are necessary ingredients in the revelatory act. To say that the "words of Amos," for example, are the "Word of God" is not to describe authorial alternatives, but to speak of the "words of Amos" as having a certain value or significance for a religious person or community. Similarly, when biblical authors write something like "And the Lord said to me. . ." the event to which they are referring is not an empirical, auditory event, but their personal appreciation or assessment that what they are writing is an expression of or conforms to God's intention for the authors' audiences. Thus, all that "the Bible *is* the Word of God" can intelligibly mean is that some regard "the Bible *as* the Word of God."[9] Such a perspective both allows and requires the reader/auditor to be selective and critical, and at the same time open to being addressed, that is, to being inspired by the power of the texts.[10]

[3] The third example of this category mistake with respect to the Bible is the appeal to the divine-promise or divine-command language transmitted by biblical authors as a basis for legitimating contemporary political judgments. As noted above, when a biblical text says that God "commanded" or "promised," it is not recording an empirical or auditory event. Such language reports, rather, the personal/communal appreciation, assessment, or interpretation of the judgment or contemplated action in question as conforming to God's intention for the author or the people. Divine-promise language

expresses the value or significance with which the author views the events in his or her life. Consider, for example, God's promise of the land to Abraham and his descendants [Genesis 13:14–17; 15:18–21]. This cannot be read literally as history, that is, as the record of an ordinarily historical event. To do so ignores the relativity and the historically conditioned nature of the text, and is logically incoherent. Divine-promise language, as all religious and theological discourse, must be regarded as metaphorical, non-literal, and essentially imaginative expressions of the life-situation of the speaker. Thus, those biblical texts which speak of the divine promise assert nothing about God's action, but do disclose the way in which ancient Hebrew authors, the redactors, and the communities that transmitted and utilized the texts interpreted their historical experience. Viewing such language as metaphorical, the work of the constructive theological imagination, means that its principle subject matter is the evaluating experience of the community. The historical event to which it refers is the act or process of ancient Israel's self-clarification in response to the sense of ultimate meaning.

It does not follow, however, that viewing divine-promise language as self-clarifying commits one to regarding such language as arbitrary, or wholly subjective. To speak religiously is to construe one's experience in a particular way. To speak religiously is to acknowledge, on the one hand, that an element of ambiguity is always present, and yet, on the other hand, that certain features of the experience can provide appropriate warrant for a construal that recognizes a transcendent reality, "signals" or "rumors,"[11] or "dimensions of ultimacy."[12] No such warrants are, however, perspicuous; they always retain their character as theological construction. Approaching the Genesis narratives of the divine promise of the land "to Abraham and to his seed forever" in this way need not undermine biblical authority; such a move simply relocates it by attaching full significance to the historical, cultural, and communal contexts out of which the Bible has emerged. The ability of the text to disclose salvific power is not compromised in such an approach, for the metaphors of divine promise can be regarded as ways of conceptualizing the surprisingly gracious experiences of liberation, of empowerment, and of communal formation. That is authority enough. They are windows on the world, but not transcriptions of divine address. Recognizing the metaphorical character of divine-promise language should thus prevent one from drawing contemporary political conclusions from the biblical narratives, or regarding them, for example, as a charter for modern state boundaries.

To argue for the political relevance of a biblically informed faith stems from an intuition consistent, in the deepest sense, with the foundational Jewish and Christian insights. These traditions have always insisted on an inescapable ethical corollary of faith, although discovering the appropriate content of this corollary is not a simple matter, save for the imperative of compassion for the stranger and justice for the oppressed. Jews and Christians may and do differ between each other and among themselves with respect to ascertaining religiously sensitive strategies to further human well-being, but neither Jew nor Christian can find in the Bible precedents adequate for contemporary political, social, or economic requirements. Both Jew and Christian should, nevertheless, be assisted in this venture of finding the best ways in which to live with or alongside one another in the *polis* by respecting the distinctive category of religious statements. There may be other, perhaps more pragmatic reasons that could lead one to refrain from a literal application of biblical images to the contemporary scene, but a respect for the peculiarity of religious language will almost certainly discourage one from moving so easily from the faith and history of ancient Israel or the early Church to an assessment of present political dilemmas and how they are to be resolved. Claims to the land might be justified in several ways, but it is illegitimate to do so by giving a literal, non-metaphorical reading of the divine-promise narratives that ignores both the character of religious discourse and what we know about how the texts in question were formed. Respect for the self-clarifying experiential base of those texts that speak of God's promise of the land "to Abraham and to his seed forever" might have a therapeutic effect on the conflict between Palestinian Jews and Arabs.[13]

2. CONSTRAINTS ON BIBLICAL AUTHORITY

The kind of authority that we can reasonably accord the Bible as a whole, or particular books or passages, must take into account, and be consistent with what we know about the character of the Bible: its authorship and textual history; the process by which its content was selected and arranged; the criteria, insofar as these can be discerned, on the basis of which writings of diverse sorts were included or excluded; and the continuing necessity of translation. This information has been available for a very long time, and should be familiar to anyone with a modern seminary education, or who has been instructed by those who have.

These widely recognized characteristics of biblical literature can be simply stated. They ought not to be regarded as controversial, nor are they debatable in the way that what were once called "the assured results" of biblical criticism was open to revision. They are, rather, the necessary conditions for all responsible criticism and for all responsible theological and religious employment. Unless they are factored into our use of the Bible, people may be misled into making a serious category mistake, and their religious affections falsely based.

Many who take the Bible seriously regard it as a source of divine revelation, and its writing and transmission as effects of divine inspiration.[14] Such revelation and inspiration, however, cannot meaningfully ignore or override the irreducible factors which have produced the texts at hand. The religious consequence of fully appreciating these factors is to recognize the Bible as one of the earthen vessels in which the gospel treasure is conveyed. To value the Bible without appreciating the humanity of its speech is to adopt a docetism with respect to the biblical texts that is just as heretical as the docetism that fails to appreciate the humanity of the person of Christ.

Seven features of the biblical texts place constraints on the kind of authority that can be responsibly granted them. Such provisional authority should be adequate grounding for core doctrine, for religious devotion, and for life-enhancing ethical recommendations. Indeed, such doctrine, devotion, and moral considerations can be preserved from being religious idiosyncrasies if and only if our valuing of their sources respects with utmost honesty what we do in fact know about them. Such respect demands of us that we bring this knowledge, already at hand, to the forefront of our consciousness, and that we let our interpretive strategies be informed by this knowledge. Naming these publicly recognizable features of the biblical texts is the first step in moving beyond the conflict over biblical authority.

[a] *Scholars determine the text*.[15] Although many more manuscripts of the Bible have survived, either as whole "books," or in fragments, than of almost all of the great classical texts of ancient Greece and Rome, we do not have access to any of the biblical autographa. Scholars use a variety of methodologies to establish the most probable original wording, to attend to the multiple manuscript traditions, their copying and transmission history, and the assessment of newly discovered manuscripts. Many parts of the Bible have a fairly stable history of textual transmission, but modern scholars must always deal with the great many textual variants. Their presence should, in principle, warn us against being absolutely confident about any particular reading.

We need, thus, to pay attention to the religious implications of the marginal comments in most modern editions. Consider, for example, the comments in *The HarperCollins Study Bible [NRSV]*[16]: "meaning is uncertain," "or. . . ," "other ancient authorities read," "add," ". . . lack." And, of course, there is the issue of the several possible endings of the *Gospel according to Mark*: 16:8; the shorter ending, or the shorter ending plus verses 9–10 [the longer ending], and the longer ending by itself, which has variants as well. And a better or more complicating manuscript may always turn up in some cave, dig, desert, or monastery library.

[b] *The texts must be translated*. Few of us read well the Hebrew, Greek, and Aramaic in which the texts were originally written. These are, for the

most part, non-living languages. Although biblical Hebrew and biblical Greek are not dissimilar from their contemporary analogues, there are no significant communities whose members speak and write these ancient languages as they once were used. Modern Hebrew, Greek, and Aramaic readers still have a translation task to do. Translation is always interpretive, and requires choices to be made.

A few examples will illustrate the kind of issues that are at stake in translating the biblical texts. [i] Is *doulos* better translated "servant" or "slave?" [ii] Is *rasah* in the Decalogue [Ex. 20:13], better translated as "do no murder," [in the usage of the Anglican *Book of Common Prayer*] or "do not kill?"[17] [iii] Consider, as well, the mischief created for generations with the translation of *diaconon* with respect to Phoebe [Rom. 16:1] as "deaconess" rather than as "deacon" or "minister," the identical terminology being used of men in the Pastoral Letters. [iv] What is the best way to translate Genesis 1:1? "In the beginning when God created the heavens and the earth," or "When God began to create. . . ," or "In the beginning God created. . . ," or "In the beginning of creation, when God made heaven and earth.?" The differences in the understanding of the doctrine of creation implied in these several options are not insignificant. [v] Notice also what the NRSV translators had to do to carry out their program of using gender-inclusive language: "sons" becomes "sons and daughters," and "brothers" becomes "brothers and sisters" when it is *decided* that the original context refers to both women and men. No one supposes that rendering an ancient text in contemporary American English idiom is a simple task, free of subjective elements.

[c.1] *The Bible is historically conditioned*, as are all literary documents. Its world-view, with a three-storied universe, is pre-scientific, and we know it to be false. Its social system is male-dominant, accepting both polygamy and slavery. It presents unacceptable models for the moral life, endorsed or tolerated then, but no longer approved; e.g., the offer of Lot's daughters [Gen. 19:8], the murder of Jepthah's daughter [Judges 11:34–40], the near murder of Isaac [Gen. 22]. Its orientation reflects throughout a heterosexual paradigm. Non-sexist exceptions are occasionally present, and we are helped to identify them with the aid of lenses that have a feminist and gay sensibility: the bonding of Ruth and Naomi, of David and Jonathan; the primeval equality in the Garden; the erotic mutuality in the Song of Songs. To take full measure of just how subversive such passages as these are of the dominant biblical assumptions, we need to appropriate the historical relativity of all the material assembled in the Bible, and of the editing and canonizing process as well.

The recognition that all the texts of the biblical anthology are historically conditioned and with that limitation able, nonetheless, or perhaps by virtue of that condition, to mediate life-enhancing power is, of course, not a new insistence. John Henry Newman, in a way quite remarkable for an early nineteenth century author, was able to affirm the truth of the apostolic revelation, and at the same time to both recognize and embrace what he identified as the "unsystematic," "irregular," "immethodical," "indirect," "covert" character of biblical writing.[18] Newman was one of the first voices to find genuine religious value in the Bible's composition history, as it was known then, acknowledging, on the one hand, that it is "the work of various independent minds in various times and places, and under various circumstances,"[19] while, on the other hand, finding "that in spite of its human form, it has in it the spirit and mind of God."[20]

> Whatever else is true about it, this is true, - that we may speak of the history, or mode of its composition, as truly as that of other books; we may speak of its writers having an object in view, being influenced by circumstances, being anxious, taking pains, purposely omitting or introducing things, supplying what others had left, or leaving things incomplete. Though the Bible be inspired, it has all such characteristics as might attach to a book uninspired,—the characteristics of dialect and style, the distinct effects of time and places, youth and age, of moral and intellectual character.[21]

Given the state of knowledge at that time about textual formation and transmission, Newman was not able to go quite so far as to speak explicitly of self-correction as a strategy discernible in the text. That will have to wait for a more informed scholarly consensus than existed in his time. Newman's approach is, nonetheless, clearly anticipatory, building, as he does, on two important and closely related principles. The first is the "principle of reserve," that is, the necessity of recognizing the limits of theological language, since that language always contains an indirect or analogous element.[22] The second is the recognition that the deposit of faith is the "living idea," and as such is open to and requires conceptual elaboration. Just as the conversion Newman recounts in the *Apologia* is a process of gradual discernment, and just as the articulation of the content of Christian believing is a process of gradual development, so biblical interpretation is a continuing process of discernment, clarification, and extrapolation. "This world of thought is the expansion of a few words, uttered, as if casually, by the fishermen of Galilee."[23] According to Newman, such a "casual" utterance is accompanied by the casual nature of the biblical texts themselves.

> . . . Scripture is not one book; it is a great number of writings, of various persons, living at different times, put together into one, and assuming its existing form as if casually and by accident. It is as if you were to seize the papers or cor-

respondence of leading men in any school of philosophy or science, which were never designed for publication, and bring them out in one volume. You would find probably in the collection so resulting many papers begun and not finished; some parts systematic and didactic, but the greater part made up of hints or of notions, which assumed first principles instead of asserting them, or of discussions upon particular points which happened to call for their attention. I say the doctrines, the first principles, the rules, the objects of the school, would be taken for granted, alluded to, implied, not stated. You would have some trouble to get at them; you would have many repetitions, many hiatuses, many things which looked like contradictions; you would have to work your way through heterogeneous materials, and after your best efforts there would be much hopelessly obscure. . . .[24]

The very nature of the biblical texts thus requires us always to distinguish between the content of revelation and the historically conditioned manner in which it is conveyed. This awareness gave Newman the freedom to attend seriously to the Bible, but not uncritically.

Many persons in the last century have called our attention to the necessity of taking with utmost seriousness the historically conditioned character of the biblical writings, considering such things as the Bible's pre-scientific worldview, geostatic cosmology, patriarchal socio-economic systems, androcentric and heterosexist consciousness. Following out leads adumbrated by Newman, they have proposed strategies for dealing with the radical difference between the view of reality presupposed and expressed by all of the biblical authors, and that of a modern, scientifically informed consciousness.

John Shelby Spong, sometime bishop of the Episcopal Diocese of Newark, dares, as he says, "to take seriously the scholarly teaching function of the episcopate,"[25] and in his work has been concerned to expose the fallacy of the fundamentalist hermeneutic of the Bible. Insofar as any ecclesial sponsor of Christian faith is wedded to biblical inerrancy, its credibility, he claims, is seriously subverted, and its ability to be a vehicle of grace is diminished. Consequently, he has sought to make the current status of biblical scholarship "available in an understandable form to the average lay person . . ." and "to place the biblical and theological debates that are commonplace among scholars at the disposal of the typical churchgoer."[26]

Harry Emerson Fosdick was engaged in a similar project in an earlier generation, employing evolutionary categories to demonstrate the continuing availability of the "abiding experiences" of the biblical vision.[27] Rudolf Bultmann chose an existentialist vehicle to enable the Christian claim to be heard in a demythologized context.[28] But it is another Anglican bishop, John Robinson, whose widely read *Honest to God*,[29] drawing heavily on Paul Tillich"s image of God as the "ground of being," comes the closest, formally speaking, to Bishop Spong's project. Yet the focus of Fosdick, Bultmann, and Robinson seems to be on the incommensurability of the biblical and contemporary world pictures and the metaphysical underpinnings of these world views. Spong's *Rescuing the Bible from Fundamentalism* shares this interest in its own way, but Spong's reading of the Bible in the light of contemporary understanding is distinguished by his explicit appropriation of the revolutionary insights of feminist biblical scholarship. His sensitivity to gender and sexual issues may help to account for the passion with which his fundamentalist critics have attacked his work, and which others have found destructive of a proper religious affection for the text.[30]

Spong claims no originality for the scholarly conclusions and insights that he transmits in his work. No one who has an historical-critical theological education should be surprised by any of Spong's scholarly judgments, although they may have devised different ways of dealing with these data. But it is Spong's suggestions about the Pauline biography that has been found to be so subversive by some of these critics.

[c.2] *Ambiguity in Paul.* In his authentic letters, and in a careful reading of Luke's account in Acts, we are given some biographical information about Paul: birthplace, education, citizenship, language facility, religious convictions, peak experiences, occupation, career plans. Paul himself also tells us that he was plagued throughout his life with a problem so troubling that he referred to it with a startling and extravagant metaphor, as a *skolops te sarki,* a "thorn in the flesh." [II Corinthians 12:7] He repeatedly sought deliverance from it in prayer, but to no avail, receiving instead an assurance of grace that enabled him to live with his problem without being immobilized, and without having his ardor for the work of the gospel diminished. But Paul never identifies just what this problem was.

Commentators have been intrigued by this strange ambiguity from the period of the early church to the present, and have speculated about the identity of this "thorn in the flesh."[31] Among the most frequently cited possibilities are malaria, epilepsy, ophthalmia, and a speech defect, all of which assume that Paul is referring to some physical ailment. The majority of commentators opt for one or another of these physiological suggestions,[32] although others think Paul might be alluding either to his being the victim of persecutions,[33] possibly a reference to a personal opponent,[34] or to "the resistance of Israel's brothers 'according to the flesh,' to the Christian faith."[35] A different area of conjecture has to do with personal anxiety, perhaps the torment of sexual temptation. Furnish identifies this as a common understanding in the Middle Ages,[36] stemming possibly from the Vulgate translation of the phrase in question as *stimulus carnis.*[37] Although Furnish thinks that Paul's desiring others to be as he is [I Corinthians 7:7] points to a successfully celibate life, the language could more easily mean simply being single or a widower. In either case, the personal anxiety remains. We shall never be sure, as Wayne Meeks reminds us, for "Paul gives metaphors rather than describing symptoms," and so "the puzzle is not likely to be solved."[38]

It is quite clear that the data give no grounds for making a firm diagnosis of Paul's medical condition, that is, for finally reducing the ambiguity of Paul's problem. Suppose, however, one took a different approach, concentrating not on what we might surmise about Paul's physical health, but on the attitude toward self and physicality, toward the possibilities of self-control and moral achievement, bearing in mind Lightfoot's observation that the condition troubling Paul was one which was liable to expose him "to contempt and ridicule."[39] This is the approach taken by John Spong, and, in an earlier generation, by Arthur Darby Nock,[40] both of whom found that taking seriously the question of sexuality sheds important light on what Paul tells us about his existential dilemma. A brief review of their projects will help to demonstrate just how unhelpful the literalist view of biblical authority really is in dealing with such examples of textual ambiguity.

Paul's view of the relationship of law and grace is conventionally understood in a displacement rather than a dialectical mode.[41] In such a view, Torah can have a preliminary usefulness, but it is has no saving power: "Now it is evident that no one is justified before God by the law." [Galatians 3:11]. "The only thing that counts is faith working through love." {Galatians 4:16] Paul gives personal testimony to the bankruptcy of his attempts to heal the distress in his life, to establish himself in right relationship with God and other people by carefully following the law. His failure in this project was not the result of his trying, for his life as a Pharisee was irreproachable. [Philippians 3:6] The failure was due to the very nature of an ethic or life policy based on law. This means, according to Nock, that we should look to Paul's experience with the law for clues concerning his trouble. We will discover, then, that the "point of difficulty for him perhaps lay in sexual desire."[42]

> Those who observed the law were as conscious as other men of moral struggle, particularly of the struggle against sins of impurity in act and thought. These sins and many others were explained as being due to an "evil instinct" implanted in man. ... Rabbinic teaching consistently maintained that the study of the Law was the most antiseptic way of diverting the mind from this and overcoming desire.[43]

In describing the moral climate of a Hellenistic Jewish perspective with which Paul would have been familiar, Nock calls attention to 4 Maccabees, an address commemorating the re-dedication of the Temple. The theme of that lecture or address is the power of "devout reason," when strengthened in the law, to be "sovereign over the emotions." [4 Maccabees 1:1, 17]. The first example the author gives is significantly that of Joseph declining the advances of Potiphar's wife.

And why is it amazing that the desires of the mind for the enjoyment of beauty are rendered powerless? It is for this reason, certainly, that the temperate Joseph is praised, because by mental effort he overcame sexual desire. For when he was young and in his prime for intercourse, by his reason he nullified the frenzy of the passions. Not only is reason proved to rule over the frenzied orgy of sexual desire, but also over every desire. [4 Maccabees 2:1–4]

Spong draws on much of the same data, but takes even more seriously than Nock Paul's description of his inner conflict and sense of guilt. He then proceeds to suggest how seeing the form of sexual desire that was so troubling to Paul to be same-sex attraction illuminates both Paul's sense of unworthiness and his appreciation of the grace which enabled him to live with his difficulty.[44] A key element in considering Paul's situation is the knowledge of how homosexuality was understood in that pre-scientific and heterosexist culture. No one in the ancient world knew anything about the modern distinction between sexual nature or orientation, on the one hand, and sexual activity, preference or life-style, and self-understanding, on the other hand. All modern thinking about sexuality regards these distinctions as absolutely central Although judgments differ on the relative importance of genetic, social, and psychological factors in establishing one's sexual orientation, all agree that this is set so firmly at such an early age that one does not have any sense of choice with respect to the object of sexual desire. One can choose only how one shall act. On the basis of the heterosexist model of the ancient world, same-sex attraction and activity would have been viewed as willed aberrations.[45] If one's sexual orientation is not, in fact, however, a matter of choice, the anxiety created by trying to control sexual desire by "devout reason" informed by the law is easy to understand. The pain Paul experienced became even greater by virtue of the peculiar theological overlay that he gave to same-sex attraction. It is never a mutual, loving relationship, but is always irrational lust, and all this [the desire, not the act as such] he holds to be divine punishment.

Therefore God gave them up in the lust of their hearts to impurity. . . . For this reason God gave them up to degrading passions. Their women exchanged natural intercourse for unnatural, and in the same way also the men, giving up natural intercourse with women, were consumed with passion for one another. Men committed shameless acts with men and received in their own persons the due penalty for their error. [Romans 1:24, 26–27].

If Paul had same-sex attraction and desire, and if he understood himself bound to the Levitical proscription of same-sex activity as a violation of Jewish cultus [Leviticus 18:22], and, further, if he knew that sexual desire cannot be regulated by will or reason, then we should be able to understand his assessment of the situation as divine punishment. Spong concludes, "If homosexuality could be viewed by Paul as God's punishment, could not whatever it was that ate at Paul's soul also be seen that way?"[46] What Spong has shown is the way familiar or neglected evidence is rendered newly visible when examined with the power of a new lens. The lens of gay awareness, fully informed by contemporary scientific understanding, helps to make sense of the range of biographical data about Paul in a disclosive manner, although we need to keep in mind the conclusion of the commentator who said about this matter, "No firm decision is possible."[47]

All of this makes honest biblical interpretation difficult, and makes it implausible to regard the biblical texts as infallible, given, in this case, their contradiction by contemporary historical and scientific knowledge. It does not, however, in itself, necessarily or completely nullify the possibility of biblical inerrancy. Biblical inerrancy is shown to be untenable by the witness of the texts themselves, and it is to a consideration of this factor, and other constraints on biblical authority, that we now turn.

[d] *Biblical truth claims vary with respect to genre.* The writings collected in the Bible display a great variety of genres, both among and within the several books. The contrast is not simply between "poetry" and "prose," for that distinction obscures the extraordinary heterogeneity of ways in which language is used in this literature. We find dreams, visions, apocalypses, laments, sagas, romances, love songs, court records, dynastic lists, letters, chronicles, midrashim, treaties, genealogies, battle plans, hymns, cultic formulae, oaths, execrations, folk-tales—and this just begins the list.

Very little biblical writing is in the form of propositions for whose truth or falsity ordinary historical or empirical evidence could be adduced. Truth indeed is conveyed in this literature, but the possibility and kind of truth varies according to the literary form, and clarity with respect to the nature of these forms is not easily achieved. When genres are confused, religious or theological mischief follows: [a] the creation hymn [Genesis 1] is heard as an account of cosmological origins, a "creationist" alternative to the evolutionary hypothesis; [b] the divine promise to Abraham is read historically as a land grant with contemporary political meaning; [c] the Christological programs of the genealogies in Matthew and Luke are read as if they were conveying ordinary biographical information. These and similar mistakes can be avoided if due regard is paid to the genre of the passage at hand. And in all such confusion the metaphorical character of religious language is lost or ignored.

Whenever particular metaphors become privileged, and their historically conditioned character forgotten, their ability to sponsor healthy, non-oppressive life options is diminished.

[e] *Biblical meaning varies with respect to the order of the contents of the Bible.*[48] A long-standing interpretive concern in working with the Bible has been to avoid taking a verse or passage or word "out of context," for the context can give us a clue as to the more original meaning of the text at hand. The notion of "context," however, must not be understood in a narrow sense, but so expanded as to include not only the setting of a passage in a book, but the books in relation to each other.[49]

The importance such ordering can have is suggested by the several issues having to do with the Old and New Testaments, and the relation of the Old Testament to the Hebrew Scriptures. As is well-known, the Jewish biblical canon is a three-part anthology: instruction or Law [Torah], Prophets [Neviim], and Writings [Kethuvim]. This order attests to the prescriptive character of the Law as the interpretive clue for the canon. The Torah is announced; the Prophets recall the people to Torah, and the Writings attest to the universal expression of the Torah. The Jewish canon concludes with II Chronicles. Here the Persian ruler Cyrus allows the exiled Judeans now living in Babylon to return to Judea, rebuild the Temple, and reinstitute the Torah as their national constitution. So the Jewish Bible [the Hebrew Scriptures] concludes "by pointing to a return to the original beginning under God's law, urging the community to try again to renew its national life lived through the Torah in [what they understood to be] "their promised land."[50]

The structure of the Old Testament canon is significantly different. The texts are arranged here with an implicit temporal sequence, with the prophetic writings at the end. This arrangement ends with Malachi's prophecy, a forward-looking anticipation of a new divine act, not a return to a vision of the people living under the Law in the land. This means that the Old Testament and the Hebrew Scriptures [the Tanak] are really two quite different books, although much of the contained material is the same. By its structure the Jewish Bible declares that it is complete in itself; by its structure the Old Testament declares an openness to God's action in the future. As Roland Murphy has observed, ". . . the Hebrew Bible is given a new canonical shape by reason of its being included with a New Testament in a canon that is broader than that of Jewish tradition."[51] Thus, the texts of the Hebrew Bible acquire new meaning when they are ordered according to the Septuagint tradition, ending with Malachi, and conjoined to the New Testament.[52]

[f] *The Bible contains conflicts and errors.* The Bible contains instances of theological conflict and contradiction [e.g., different instructions about how many animals Noah should take into the ark: two of every kind [Gen. 6:19],

or seven pairs of all clean animals [Gen. 7:2]; opposing views on the adoption of a monarchical system in ancient Israel; Amos' indictment of the very feasts and festivals presumably prescribed elsewhere in the Torah]. The Bible also includes mistakes [e.g., "See, I am sending my messenger ahead of you . . ." is from Malachi, not Isaiah, as Mark states {Mk. 1:2]. Again, Ahimelech, not Abiathar, as noted in Mk. 2:26, was high priest when David ate the consecrated bread.] Now most of these factual errors are of marginal significance with respect to the ability of the Bible to clarify what is amiss in the human situation, and to announce the divine strategy for our personal and social renovation. But the presence of any mistakes, however unimportant, and of more than occasional textual uncertainties, should warn us against making an uncritical investment in biblical authority. We ought not to confuse the saving acts of God with the language in which the good news has been transmitted to us.

[g] *The Bible is self-revising*. Its plurality of views cannot be credibly harmonized, for they often present contradictory not just supplementary traditions [e.g., the birth and infancy narratives in Matthew and Luke]. This corrective, altering, or revising process is evident both in the development of the Western Text of the New Testament, for example, and in the final, canonical form of many of the documents.

Sometimes the self-revising character of the Bible is seen in the way an earlier emphasis or metaphor is modified or replaced. We can see such a development in the movement from the earliest to the latest of the gospels. As is well-known, each of the canonical gospels reflects a distinct Christology: Jesus as a divinely acknowledge herald of the new age [Mark], an instructor of a new moral way [Matthew], an exemplar of a new way of life [Luke], the human embodiment of the divine [John]. By transmitting the Synoptic Gospels along with John as a four-fold gospel, so to speak, the final editors show how the full implications of belief in the extraordinariness of Jesus of Nazareth was not fully worked out at first, but developed over time.

The credibility of the literalist hermeneutic collapses in the light of the redaction history of the texts. We know enough about the composition and canonical process to recognize that the texts which the literalists believe to be without error were not so regarded by the biblical authors themselves and those responsible for shaping the documents in the forms in which they have been transmitted to us. The history of the Western Text of the New Testament discloses not only the freedom that its shapers exhibited to "correct," that is, to alter and revise, but also something of the various theological agendas that informed such a corrective process. Several New Testament scholars have identified the ways in which the intentional changes in the text display such programs as the downplaying of Christianity's Jewish roots[53] and exalting the person and function of Peter, but the modification strategy that is especially significant is the anti-female or anti-feminist bias that is effected by occasional word changes.[54] Some of the most significant of these changes include the following: [1] Acts 17:4—changing *gunaikes* to *gunaikon* so that the women of prominence in the community become simply wives of leading citizens; [2] Acts 17—changing references to Aquila and Priscilla, so that his name could come before hers, speaking of Priscilla simply as a spouse rather than as a co-worker or missionary; or by dropping Priscilla's name altogether; [3] Colossians 4:1–5—replacing "Nympha and the church in her house" with "Nymphas and the church in his house."[55]

That there are differences and contradictions in the texts is, thus, no modern discovery, but we are in a position, as previous generations were not, to take measure of those textual vagaries in such a way as to devise a hermeneutic informed by the dynamic of biblical authorship itself. Not to do so, in the face of such knowledge, is to be blind, perverse, or dishonest.

Those who defend the inerrancy of the texts sometimes resist the methods and conclusions of historical-critical scholarship by suggesting that such a perspective is alien to these texts, or to texts of this sort, and invariably reads the texts in the light of modern concerns, or imposes onto the texts contemporary conclusions inconsistent with the original intent of the biblical authors. But these authors themselves are shown by the redaction history and the process of textual formation and transmission, to take a corrective approach to inherited materials. Thus the Bible itself opposes its being understood as an inerrant canon.[56]

I want now to identify some examples of just how the redaction of a text makes a literalist hermeneutic not only inappropriate but impossible. What we will see is how one author revises a text that had important valence in the religious community, not so much to improve linguistic style, to transmit an alternate or supplementary tradition, or to extend a reference, but to reduce ambiguity, alter a theological emphasis, correct a doctrinal affirmation, or to change communal instructions. In each case, by his or her literary act, the redactor is saying that the text at hand is fallible, inadequate, or incorrect. The redaction process itself, thus, makes it impossible for us to regard the biblical texts as free from error.[57]

[i] The fifth century BCE priests had at hand the Yahwist's creation narrative, in which the relation between male and female is not unambiguous. In that narrative [Genesis 2:4–3:24] *ha adam*, the earth creature, is set to live in the garden, but his existential loneliness is so problematic that Yahweh creates a partner for him, with whom he can be vis-à-vis. [The other animals cannot provide satisfactory companionship.] But although *ha adam* is referred to in male terms, *ha adam* does not become sexually differentiated until the

woman is created, at which time *ha adam* becomes *ish* and *ishshah*. Thus humankind becomes male and female at the same time. The egalitarian partnership they share is destroyed by their refusal to live in the garden on the basis of the terms on which life was given to them, and the original equality is then replaced by a pattern of dominance and submission.

To reinforce the divine intention of mutuality presupposed in this tenth century narrative, and to reduce its ambiguity, the priestly editors juxtaposed that folk-tale with a sophisticated Sabbath-oriented creation poem [Genesis 1:1–2:3], in which the equality of man and woman is unmistakably affirmed: "Then God said, 'Let us make humankind {*adam*} in our image, according to our likeness.' . . . So God created humankind {*adam*} in his image, in the image of God he created them {him}, male and female he created them. [Genesis 1:26–27 – NRSV].

Sometimes the self-revising effect of the authors/editors is the subtle consequence of the juxtaposition of different traditions: "God saw everything that he had made, and indeed *it was very good*." [Genesis 1:31], but "Then the Lord God said, '*It is not good* that the man should be alone . . .'" [Genesis 2:18]

The opening chapters of the Bible thus transmit traditions which disclose a process in which texts are transformed, a process which thus makes questionable a literalist hermeneutic.

{ii} Sometimes the redactors have woven together or juxtaposed alternative, conflicting versions of an event. The accounts in I Samuel of the decision of the Twelve Tribe Confederation to become a monarchy with Saul as king are an example of such a conflation. The older tradition, the "Saul source," [I Samuel 8:1–10, etc.] views the royalist achievement as reflecting the divine intention for Israel. Samuel endorses the change [9:19–74], and is pleased with the choice of Saul. The later tradition, the "Samuel source," [I Samuel 9:1–11, etc.] views the royalist movement as a betrayal of Yahweh's rule in Israel. Samuel warns the people of the problematic consequences of Israel's developing political institutions like all the other nations, and agrees with great reluctance to anoint Saul, a concession to their blindness. This later tradition corrects the affirmative attitude toward kingship reflected in the earlier tradition. The later redactor, reflecting a shift of consciousness in the post-Solomonic era, wove the two sources together, and in so doing was able to suggest a strategy for holding to the congruence of the problematic monarchy with the will of Yahweh, so long as that institution is set in the framework of the prophetic critique of idolatry. Such a procedure, however, cannot obscure the judgment of the source sympathetic to Samuel that the witness of the Saul source, taken in itself, was incorrect.

{iii} Sometimes the correction or revision is a perspectival shift that is not contained in the final form of a single text, but is evident in the inclusion by the final shapers of the canon of an earlier doctrinal and liturgical prescription together with its later rejection. Leviticus 1–7 provides detailed regulations concerning the regimen of burnt animal and grain offerings to which a post-wilderness Israel understood itself to be bound. Such a system was explained as a way of dealing with Israel's having moved beyond the desert mode of life in which the direct relationship with God made such sacrifices unnecessary and irrelevant. But the eighth century prophets were more than skeptical of the religious efficacy of the sacrificial system; they condemned the practice altogether. Amos inveighed against the Temple cultus in clear, unmistakable terms:

> I hate, I despise your festivals,
>   and I take no delight in your solemn assemblies.
> Even though you offer me burnt offerings
>   and grain offerings,
> I will not accept them,
>   and the offerings of well-being of your
>   fatted animals
> I will not look upon.
> Tale away from me the noise of your songs.
> I will not listen to the melody of your harps.
> But let justice roll down like waters,
> and righteousness like an everflowing stream.
>   [Amos 5:21–24, NRSV]

Micah's dismissal of the appropriateness of the Levitical requirement is just as explicit:

> With what shall I come before the Lord,
>   and bow myself before God on high?
> Shall I come before him with burnt offerings,
>   with calves a year old?
> Shall I give my firstborn for my transgression,
>   the fruit of my body for the sin of my soul?
> He has told you, O mortal, what is good;
>   and what does the Lord require of you
> but to do justice, and to love kindness,
>   and to walk humbly with your God?
>   [Micah 6:6–8, NRSV]

Leviticus and the prophets cannot both be correct.

We could, of course, consider these contradictory views of burnt animal and grain offerings as but two stages in a developing religious expression, evolving from a ritualistic to a more explicitly ethical focus. Although religious traditions may admit of change and other forms of development [a later form, for example, making explicit some idea or practice that was only implicit at the beginning], a simple application of an evolutionary paradigm should be avoided, since it conveys a sense of movement from a "lower" to a "higher" form of religious expression. We seek here only to describe or to name a change which the authors effected as a correction, not to pass judgment on the value of the change. One could regard the canonical context of these contradictory voices simply as the preservation of two historically conditioned understandings of the divine requirement. The canonical process, however, was not simply a matter of collecting and transmitting, but a selective activity which required judgments about a text's importance and consistency with the mandates of the covenant. It is enough here simply to call attention to the fact of correction, without presuming to pass judgment on the appropriateness of the change. No matter how the change is accounted for, the change made by the authors/redactors functions as a correction, certainly a revision. The relativity of the biblical witnesses is consequently affirmed, and the fundamentalist or literalist claim to biblical inerrancy is shown once again to be indefensible on the basis of the nature of the texts themselves.

{iv} Sometimes the correction occurs within a single text whose present form is traditionally attributed to a single author. One example of such a variance is Paul's recommendation in I Corinthians of proper attire for those leading in public worship of the Christian assemblies. "Any woman," he wrote, "who prays or prophesies with her head unveiled disgraces her head." [I Corinthians 11:5]. This puzzling, culture-specific directive is, implicitly, either ignored or rejected later when the author advises that "women should be silent in the churches. For they are not permitted to speak. . . ." [I Corinthians 14:33b-36]. The language about liturgical attire clearly presupposes precisely the pastoral situation which the later passage claims is not allowed. Either Paul changed his mind, or, as most scholars conclude, the later prohibition is an interpolation from some unknown hand, writing in Paul's name, from the time in which the originally egalitarian communities had begun to succumb to the general patriarchal ethos of the Mediterranean world. But in either case, the view that the biblical text is without error is ruled out by the redaction history of the present text itself, without applying any extra-biblical criterion.

{v} The clearest cases of biblical self-correction are perhaps those that reveal the Matthean and Lucan revisions of Mark.[58] [a] Mark reports that a man asks Jesus, "Good Teacher, what must I do to inherit eternal life?", to which Jesus responds by deflecting the evaluation of himself as good. "Why do you call me good? No one is good but God alone." [Mark 10:17–18] The Matthean evangelist, apparently uncomfortable with the Christology presupposed by the Markan text at hand, changes both the question and the response to suggest that Jesus regarded the encounter as an opportunity for general ethical inquiry: "'Teacher, what good deed must I do to have eternal life?' And he said to him, 'Why do you ask me about what is good? There is only one who is good . . .'" [Matthew 196–17]

[b] Mark describes the failure of Jesus' work in his hometown as the consequence of the limited nature of Jesus' power: ". . . *and he could do no deed of power there* . . . and he was amazed at their unbelief." [Mark 6:5–6]. Matthew revised the account so as to heighten Jesus' image, and to give a different accounting for his failure: "And *he did not do many deeds of power* there because of their unbelief." [Matthew 13:58]

[c] In the same way Luke seems to have felt no constraint to regard the Markan text as unassailable. In Mark's version the centurion in charge of the execution party exclaims, "Surely this man was God's Son." [Mark 15:34], thus completing the frame for the Jesus story which Mark began by announcing, "The beginning of the good news of Jesus Christ, the Son of God." [Mark 1:1] Luke, however, saw this narrative as another opportunity to follow out his apologetic interest in demonstrating the political neutrality of the developing Jesus movement. Accordingly, Luke revises Mark's statement to have the centurion exclaim, "Certainly this man was innocent." [Luke 23:47], thus reinforcing the declaration by Pilate, the representative of the Roman state, that the responsibility for the crucifixion of Jesus falls elsewhere than on Rome.

Thus it is that when we allow the Bible to tell us about itself, we learn that the authority it possesses is not that of an inerrant, infallible text. This does not mean, of course, that one may not properly call the Bible "the Word of God." Such language, however, can mean only that these venerable texts are being regarded *as* the Word of God; that is to say, the Bible has authority by virtue of individuals or communities granting some special status or importance to it. Biblical writings must always be read critically, and they must not be invested with a prescriptive power that contradicts contemporary historical and scientific knowledge. When churches fail to do this, they seriously compromise the integrity and the relevance of their message.[59]

To speak of the Bible *as* the Word of God does not mean, however, that such discourse is wholly subjective, and a matter of individual taste. Many biblical passages have an intrinsic power to illuminate, to challenge, to inform, to inspire, to comfort, to indict, etc., despite their age and historically-conditioned character. This happens whenever the reader/auditor is open to being addressed by the text. The Bible can have such authority, however, only if the reader/auditor brings to bear in his or her response all that we have learned about the nature of the world, of the human person and human society.

The kind of authority which we may reasonably grant the Bible is necessarily modified by the several constraints that we have noted in this chapter: the fact that scholars determine the texts; that the texts must be translated; that it is historically conditioned; by the ambiguity of its metaphors and several genres; by the ordering of arrangement of the texts in relation to each other; by the presence in it of conflicts and errors; and finally by its self-revising character. The necessary ambiguity of the Bible is chiefly shown by the Bible's own habit of self-correction, or self-revising—that redaction process by which biblical authors and editors themselves have witnessed to a high degree of freedom in relation to the text. The imperative that follows from this is the absolute necessity to be honest, that is, to allow those texts that can still speak significantly to us to do so, without claiming that the Bible as a whole can do so. The treasure of the divine intention for human life is, after all, contained in earthen vessels.

NOTES

1. 'Authority" is an ambiguous term, with a wide range of possible meanings and usages in this context: moral, historical, absolute, advisory, unquestioned, resource, guide, core, etc. The analysis in this chapter is concerned to show that to be intelligible, any meaning or usage must be consonant with what we do in fact know about the Bible.

2. I have elsewhere discussed in a general way the surprise of discovering that the biblical texts are sometimes puzzling or unclear and sometimes contradictory; and how such a recognition might make it easier for those suspicious of the patriarchal and heterosexist views present in the text to enter more appreciatively, if critically, into the biblical world. See "Ambiguity and Text," in my *Inquiry*, pp. 779–93. An earlier version of some of the material in this chapter appeared as "The Bible As An Earthen Vessel: A Plea for Biblical Honesty," in *Encounter* [Vol. 58:4, Autumn 1997, pp. 413–418] The present chapter is more directly concerned with the issue of "biblical authority," and the ways in which that needs to be reconceptualized, with particular attention to some ecclesial implications.

3. "The Ordination of a Priest," *The Book of Common Prayer* [New York: The Church Hymnal Corporation, 1977], p. 526. Similar affirmations are mandated by many other Christian churches.

4. "Old" and "New" are, of course, Christian categories when applied to the Bible. No theologically neutral terminology exists that is wholly satisfactory to both Jewish and Christian communities. The relevance of this issue for the question of biblical authority will be discussed later in this chapter.

5. See, for example, Amos Niven Wilder, *Theopoetic* [Philadelphia: Fortress Press, 1976]; Gordon D. Kaufman, *The Theological Imagination: Constructing the Concept of God* [Philadelphia: Westminster Pres, 1981], especially "Christian Theology as Imaginative Construction," pp. 263–279; also Sallie McFague, *Metaphorical Theol-*

ogy [Philadelphia: Fortress Press, 1982], and *Models of God* [Philadelphia: Fortress Press, 1987].

6. Stephen F. Nall, *The Advocate* Vol. 4, No. 1 [April 1991].

7. Although it is not very clear precisely what Clement meant by "spiritual" when applied to the Gospel of John, he is obviously intending a contrast with the more straight-forward, "bodily" nature of the Synoptic gospels.

8. Ted Nelson, *The Advocate*, Vol. 4, No. 1 [April 1991], p. 1.

9. In a similar vein, Tom Driver can speak of the authority of human experience as "Word of God." See Tom F. Driver, *Patterns of Grace: Human Experience as Word of God* [San Francisco: Harper and Row, 1977], especially "Human Experience Is Word of God," pp. 144–149.

10. This dialectical relationship of reader and text is explored further in my chapter, "The Bible as Icon and Idol," in *Inquiry*, pp. 127–130.

11. These terms are from Peter L. Berger, *A Rumor of Angels* [New York: Doubleday and Co., 1969], passim.

12. Langdon Gilkey, *Naming the Whirlwind* [Indianapolis: Bobbs-Merrill, 1969].

13. This issue is explored more fully in my article "The Category Mistake of Messianic Nationalism," *Arab Studies Quarterly*, Vol. 17, No. 4 [Fall 1995], pp. 1–9. The land rightly belongs to YHWH, and even with the promise it is never "given over" to Abraham. See Lev. 25:23 [NRSV]: The Lord spoke to Moses on Mount Sinai, saying "The land shall not be sold in perpetuity, for the land is mine; with me you are but aliens and tenants."

14. It is a mistake to think of *texts* rather than *authors* and endorsing *communities* as inspired. When properly considered, the Bible is sufficiently revelatory as to provide insight for our self-understanding and to charter the moral reformation of our individual and social lives.

15. I first began to attend to the serious implications of this commonplace fact by noting the comment of Elisabeth Schuessler-Fiorenza, *But She Said* [Boston: Beacon Press, 1992], p. 213, n. 14.

16. *The HarperCollins Study Bible [NRSV]*, Wayne A. Meeks, General Editor [New York: HarperCollins, 1993], *passim*.

17. This issue derives from the recognition that the commandment with respect to killing was never understood in ancient Israel as prohibiting all intentional termination of human life, as in warfare or capital punishment, for example. *Rtsh* has a wide semantic range in biblical Hebrew.

18. These adjectives appear *passim* in John Henry Newman, Lecture 3, "On the General Structure of the Bible as a Record of Faith," from Part 1, "Lectures on the Scripture Proof of the Doctrines of the Church," *Tracts for the Times* [London: J.G.F. and J. Rivington and J.H. Parker, 1840] Vol. VI, No. 85, pp. 27–34.

19. Ibid., p. 34

20. Ibid., p. 30.

21. Ibid., p. 30.

22. John Macquarrie, *Jesus Christ in Modern Thought* [Philadelphia: Trinity Press International, 1990], p. 13.

23. Newman, *University Sermons*, 1871 edition, p. 317, cited in J.M. Cameron, "Editor's Introduction," in John Henry Newman, *An Essay on the Development of Christian Doctrine*, ed. and intro. By J. M. Cameron [Baltimore: Penguin Books, 1997 4], p. 36.

24. Newman, "On the General Structure of the Bible as a Record of Faith," pp. 30–31.

25. John Shelby Spong, *Rescuing the Bible from Fundamentalism* [San Francisco: HarperSanFrancisco, 1991], p. xii.

26. Ibid., p. ix. Spong's work is not so much marked by originality of view or a ground-breaking kind of research, but by an accessible, reporting style which transmits the results of biblical scholarship to a wide audience. For that reason, I have chosen to call attention to his writing as a ready example of the range of ambiguity with which this book is concerned.

27. Harry Emerson Fosdick, *The Modern Use of the Bible* [New York: The Macmillan Company, 1924].

28. Rudolf Bultmann, *Jesus Christ and Mythology* [New York: Charles Scribner's Sons, 1958].

29. John A. T. Robinson, *Honest to God* [Philadelphia: Westminster Press, 1963].

30. See, for example, Lloyd J. Averill, "Bishop Spong's 'Rescue' of the Bible, *The Christian Century*, Vol. 108, No. 17, pp. 559–561.

31. For a review of the literature on the most frequently mentioned possibilities see Victor Paul Furnish, *II Corinthians* [Garden City: Doubleday and Co., 1984], *The Anchor Bible*, Vol. 32A, pp. 546–552; also Bengt Holmberg, *Paul and Power* [Philadelphia: Fortress Press, 1978], pp. 75–77.

32. See, e.g., Floyd V. Filson, "Introduction and Exegesis of The Second Epistle to the Corinthians" [New York: Abingdon-Cokesbury Press, 1953] *The Interpreter's Bible* Vol. 10, p. 407. Benjamin W. Robinson speaks of possible physiological difficulty in less specific terms: "Among the various explanations the view which most nearly fits Paul's references is that under special excitement he was subject to sudden attacks of violent headache or dizziness, or even fainting." *The Life of Paul* [Chicago: The University of Chicago Press, 1918]. pp. 39–40.

33. Furnish, p. 549.

34. Donald Joseph Selby, *Toward an Understanding of St. Paul* [Englewood Cliffs: Prentice-Hall, 1962], p. 145, n. 10.

35. Commentator, *The Jerusalem Bible*, Alexander Jones, general editor [Garden City: Doubleday and Co., 1966], p. NT 321, n. 12d.

36. Furnish, p. 548.

37. The early English translations continue this tradition: "unquyetness of the flesh" [Tyndale, 1525, and the Great Bible, 1539]. Michael Grant also has called attention to the fact that writers on asceticism, from the period of the Fathers of the early church on, "thought it referred to sexual temptation, and they may have been right." Michael Grant, *Saint Paul* [London: Weidenfeld and Nicolson, 1976], p. 23. Grant then refers to Arthur Darby Nock, who "although unwilling to commit himself on the meaning of the particular phrase in question, has lent his authority to this

interpretation." [p. 23] For Grant, Paul's "unmistakably pejorative attitude towards sex does raise insistent questions about his own tastes and practices," [p. 25], and Grant rejects the conventional interpretation that finds Paul's eschatological perspective determinative. For Grant the problem may well be "suppressed and frustrated sexual desire." [p. 25]

38. Wayne Meeks, *The Writings of St. Paul* [New York: W. W. Norton and Co., 1972], p. 64, n. 2.

39. Joseph B. Lightfoot, cited in Holmberg, p. 76, n. 89.

40. Arthur Darby Nock, *St. Paul* [New York: Harper and Brothers, 1937].

41. For this reason, many Jewish commentators judge that Paul seriously misunderstood the relationship of law and grace.

42. Nock, p. 71.

43. Nock. P. 71.

44. Spong outlines this speculation in *Living in Sin: A Bishop Rethinks Human Sexuality* [San Francisco: Harper & Row, 1988], pp. 149–152, and develops it in *Rescuing the Bible*, pp. 115–120. An earlier and much more oblique intimation of the possibility of Paul's same-sex orientation is found in Sholem Asch's reverently erotic description of Paul's relationship with the young Timothy, especially Asch's rendering of Timothy's being circumcised and then embraced and kissed by Paul. [Sholem Asch, *The Apostle*, tr. Maurice Samuel {New York: G. P. Putnam's Sons, 1943}, p. 373–377; see also pp. 344–345.]

45. This generalization may apply to the world of Paul's awareness and presupposition, but it does not, of course, adequately suggest the range of different meanings that have been attached to the human nature/natural/unnatural from the ancient period to our own. That one should be cautious about an "essentialist" approach follows from a rehearsal of those many voices who have regarded the male as the paradigm of human nature—Aristotle, Aquinas, Freud, to name only three of the most influential. That "natural" seems to be culture-specific is suggested by the *Dream Analysis* of Artemidoros [2nd century AD], for whom the distinction between natural and unnatural sexual acts did not depend on the sexual sameness or difference of one's partner, nor on reproductive potential, but on the preservation of social status—the ranking of superior to inferior. [For a useful discussion of Artemidoros see John J. Winkler, "Unnatural Acts: Erotic Protocols in Artemidoros' *Dream Analysis*, in *The Constraints of Desire* {New York and London: Routledge, 1990}, pp. 17–44].

46. Spong, *Living in Sin*, p. 151.

47. Commentator, *The New Oxford Annotated Bible with the Apocryphal/Deuterocanonical Books*, ed. Bruce Metzger and Roland E. Murphy, *[The New Revised Standard Version]*, [New York: Oxford University Press, 1991], p. 160NT, n. to II Corinthians 12:7.

48. See my article "Do Christians Read from the Hebrew Scriptures?," unpublished manuscript, nd.

49. The particular context at issue here is one aspect of the literary context. A fuller contextual analysis would, of course, explore the historical and social contexts, among others.

50. Moshe Gresser, "The Old Testament vs. the Tanakh," unpublished manuscript, nd.

51. Roland Murphy, "Old Testament/Tanakh—Canon and Interpretation," in Roger Brooks and John J. Collins, ed., *Hebrew Bible or Old Testament?* [Notre Dame: University of Notre Dame Press, 1990], p. 14.

52. Some scholars misjudge the terminology of "Old" and "New" Testaments as irretrievably expressive of anti-Jewish supersessionism., and an inescapable part of anti-Jewish theological rhetoric. See Elisabeth Schuessler-Fiorenza, *Jesus: Miriam's Child, Sophia's Prophet* [New York: Continuum, 1994], p. 193, n. 8. As I have shown in my article "Do Christians Read from the Hebrew Scriptures?," the Jewish tradition is better honored by acknowledging that the ordering of the books makes the Jewish Bible and the Old Testament quite different books.

53. Marcion's similar agenda was carried out in a much bolder and more thoroughgoing way than any of the emenders working on the Western Text.

54. See Bruce M. Metzger, *The Text of the New Testament: Its Transmission, Corruption, and Restoration* [New York and Oxford: Oxford University Press, 1992], third, enlarged edition, pp. 195–206, 295–297; Richard I. Pervo, "Social and Religious Aspects of the 'Western' Text," in Dennis E. Groh and Robert Jewett, eds., *The Living Text: Essays in Honor of Ernest W. Saunders* [Lanham: University Press of America, 1985], pp. 229–241; Ben Witherington, "The Anti-Feminist Tendencies of the 'Western' Text in Acts," *Journal of Biblical Literature*, Vol. 103 [1984], pp. 82–84.

55. Both Pervo, *op. cit.*, and Witherington, *op. cit.*, provide a more extensive listing of textual modifications reflecting this anti-feminist bias.

56. Several studies have explored this characteristic of the Bible. David McLain Carr, *From D to Q: A Study of Early Jewish Interpretations of Solomon's Dream at Gibeon* [Missoula: Scholars Press, 1991]. Carr identifies numerous examples of biblical writers reinterpreting and refocusing authoritative traditions for their own circumstances. Ilana Pardes, *Countertraditions in the Bible* [Cambridge: Harvard University Press, 1992], explores the heterogeneity of the Hebrew canon, and calls attention to the way in which the texts themselves disclose trends that are antithetical to and that continuously challenge the structures of patriarchy.

57. A fundamentalist interpreter is not, of course, unaware of these textual problems [here identified as contradictions and corrections], but characteristically deals with the situation by elaborate and artificial strategies of harmonization. It is the fundamentalist who imposes alien concerns onto the Bible, and fails to take seriously what the texts themselves tell us about themselves.

58. This is the example to which John Spong has appealed in his concern to show the untenability of the literalist claim. [Spong, *Rescuing the Bible*, p. 150]. My discussion, and Spong's, presuppose the adequacy of the hypothesis of Markan priority now geneally held by the community of scholars. A minority of New Testament commentators do continue to find some form of the Griesbach hypothesis of the priority of Matthew a more satisfactory basis for dealing with the Synoptic problem. [See, for example, C.S. Mann, *Mark* {Garden City: Doubleday and Co., 1986. *The Anchor Bible*, Vol. 27}]. The relevance of the synoptic examples adduced

here for the position suggested in this chapter does not, of course, depend on either hypothesis, since in both cases one evangelist is correcting the other.

59. Most Christian churches have, for a long time, developed ways of evaluating biblical injunctions that are critical, selective, and based on contemporary under-standings of the nature of the human person and human community, recognizing, for example, that such injunctions in the biblical texts are culture-specific and do not ad-mit of a simple application to modern life. We have rejected the biblical views of slav-ery, gender inequality, nudity, capital offenses, cultic regulations, and the like. Many persons, however, who recognize the relativity of these ethical and cultic prescrip-tions, still appeal to what are presumed to be biblical teachings with respect to a range of sexual issues, about which the Bible actually has very little to say [contraception, divorce, same sex activity, e.g.]. When they do so, it would appear that some other disguised, perhaps unconscious, agenda is operating in such an appeal than an inter-est simply in being "faithful to the Bible."

Chapter Three

The Man

Just as a certain ambiguity necessarily attaches to the Book whose historically-conditioned, self-correcting human words are held to convey the divine intention for human life, so a similar ambiguity belongs to the Man whose historically-conditioned life and work are held to embody the divine being and power as a resource for the renovation of human life and community. In the preceding chapter I suggested how a knowledge of the redaction history of the biblical writings, along with other constraints, discloses an ambiguity that makes a fundamentalist or literalist hermeneutic unfeasible. I aim in this chapter to suggest how an appreciation of the process or logic of the churches' evaluation of the person and career of Jesus of Nazareth discloses an ambiguity that makes a fundamentalist or literalist Christology untenable. Just as our earlier inquiry has shown something of what can be meant when we speak of the Bible *as* the Word of God, so the present inquiry will show something of what can be meant when we speak of Jesus *as* the Christ, or *as* the Son of God.

Reflecting on both the form and content of Christological affirmation is not only a continuing enterprise, but also one which has special possibilities peculiar to the present moment. Such reflection is concerned with both the meaning of the several Christological predications, and the dynamic or logic of the ascriptive process. Although the content rather than the process has received most attention, understanding the process will illuminate what the churches did in the New Testament period and in the ecumenical decisions of the fourth and fifth Christian centuries, and what Christian assemblies continue to do as they repeat that early language. Achieving clarity on this matter will uncover the ambiguity intrinsic to the churches' theological work. Appreciating this ambiguity can assist the contemporary theological effort to reformulate the churches' Christological affirmations in a new way, and will disclose the necessity of such a revisioning project.

1. THE CONTEMPORARY THEOLOGICAL CLIMATE

Three movements on the contemporary theological scene make this investigation credible in a way which would not have been possible a short generation ago. [1] The ecumenical character of the contemporary theological situation is well-known, but the ecumenical parameters are more inclusive than once was the case when the voices in the conversation were distinguished simply as Protestant, Anglican, and Roman Catholic, with an occasional Orthodox contribution. Now that discussion is enriched by the views of those writing from Hispanic, African American, Feminist, Womanist, Gay and Lesbian perspectives. Christological reconstruction will have to give serious attention to them, and to the syntactical possibilities and peculiarities of non-Indo-European languages in the necessary effort to break the theological hegemony of the North Atlantic world.

A further sign of the new ecumenical situation is the increasingly sophisticated state of the Jewish-Christian dialogue. Although the relevance of this dialogue is only beginning to be noted, its fruitfulness may be unusually important. Let me suggest why this is the case. Recent Jewish-Christian discussions have seen the diminution of both Christian triumphalism and Jewish fear of Christian aggrandizement and hostility toward Christian ideas. This development recognizes an irreducible asymmetry in the conversation. The continuation of Jewish religiousness has been problematic for Christian self-understanding very differently from the way in which Christian religiousness is problematic for Jewish self-understanding. Christians are and have been a Jewish problem sociologically, politically, and perhaps psychologically, but not theologically. Consequently, most Jewish work has been expended in the effort to ease interreligious tensions, although some Jewish scholars of an earlier generation, notably Claude Montefiore and Joseph Klausner, have made important contributions to New Testament studies. But during nearly a century of ecumenical fraternizing, the conversation partners have deepened their dialogue, discovering an openness to each being of theological significance to the other. The Christian scholar recognizes the probability of radical Christological reconstruction to which a more sophisticated discussion may lead.[1] The Jewish scholar gradually recognizes the possibility of a transformed, modified, or enriched Judaism that might ensue were something of Jesus' program for renewal recovered and incorporated into the consciousness and structures of modern Jewish religiousness. And so "Jesus" has become a problem for a distinguished group of Jewish authors [including

Lauterbach, Sandmel, Zeitlin, Schoeps, Bokser, Isaac, Cohn, Silver, Kaufman, Rosenzweig], most of whom approach the problem in a new way, avoiding the prejudging that characterized an earlier Jewish concern. The traditional voice is still heard, of course, in such Orthodox scholars as Alexander Kohanski[2], who seeks to demonstrate that Jesus was indeed a heretic, an apostate, who called for a vision that amounted to the complete subjectivization of the Mosaic revelation. Others, however, have been motivated by a desire to repatriate Jesus to Judaism, and have sought to show precisely the opposite, that Jesus as he really was is wholly compatible with some of the perspectives of pre-rabbinic Jewish religiousness. The contemporary Jewish consideration seeks to explore the early Christian and Jewish texts according to the most rigorous employment of the generally recognized canons of scientific biblical criticism, without a prior determination of what picture of Jesus one hopes will emerge. The consequence of this development is that coherent, reciprocal discussion is now possible, and a genuinely useful move in revisioning Christology may be made that could build on a non-polemical Jewish reading of Christological titles, and on a shared understanding of the peculiar ambiguity inherent in the process of Christological naming.[3]

[2] A second development which gives the present project such promise is the shift in New Testament studies away from the Bultmann era's despair of making any important distinction between the historical Jesus and the kerygmatic Christ, and even if such a distinction could be made, rejecting the kerygmatic significance of the resulting picture of the historical Jesus. To be sure, the New Testament texts themselves not only make no distinction between the historical Jesus and the kerygmatic Christ, they completely identify the remembered Jesus with the Risen Christ experienced in the community's life. Further, it is now recognized that whatever historical material is present in the canonical gospels is there not for ordinary historical reasons, but to serve the various needs of the communities for and from which the gospels were written, one of which may have been the concern to root the kerygma in the life-situation of Jesus. But New Testament scholars are now taking with new seriousness the fact that some Christian authors in the first Christian century employed [invented?] a narrative genre ostensibly biographical, not simply a homiletical or epistolary genre, to convey their theological assessment of the person and career of Jesus of Nazareth. No one suggests that the gospels are biographies, but that they contain genuine biographical data seems no longer in dispute.[4] And this judgment holds for the Johannine strata as well as the Synoptic material. Contemporary Jewish openness to the historical Jesus thus is supported by and matches the new direction which New Testament scholars and theologians have now been taking for some time.

[3] The third development which makes Christological reconstruction an especially fruitful project now is the language turn in contemporary theology, particularly the explicit recognition of the non-literal, or more precisely, the metaphorical status of the tradition's Christological discourse. That the New Testament and the conciliar designations of Jesus are not names as such but titles or honorifics is not, of course, a modern discovery. But the insistence that we take a serious theological measure of their non-literal status is new.[5] Some have begun to identify the consequences of such measuring and to show how an honest embracing of the Christological titles as context-specific metaphors can free us from the twin perils of irrelevance [given our distance from the patriarchal[6] and metaphysical[7] consciousness which originally gave birth to and nourished the metaphors], and idolatry [regarding the ascriptions as names rather than as metaphors]. We are now ready to attend seriously to the theological enterprise as constructive rather than explicative or systematic, appreciating the linguistic decisions of an earlier time as suggestions and contributions to but not as closed settlements of Christological issues. The interested Jewish participant can only be grateful for this linguistic turn. The Christian participant now characteristically says less that Jesus *is* the Christ or the Son of God, for example, and speaks more frequently of Jesus *as* the Christ, *as* the Son of God, that is, recognizes that the tensive nature of metaphor requires us to focus directly on the question of the meaning of such oblique predications, and the logic of the ascriptive process.

2. CHRISTOLOGY AND AMBIGUITY

The conventional and stereotypical way of viewing the dynamic of messianic ascription seems unaware of any ambiguity that might be present in the application of the various metaphors to the historical Jesus. It usually begins with an investigation into the way in which the several messianic titles were understood in the history and religion of ancient Israel, and then asks in what way and to what extent the historical Jesus matches one or more of these patterns of Jewish anticipation. It often takes this form: the Jewish people were looking for a Messiah to redeem Israel. Jesus came. Some Jews found that he fit the definition; others, the majority, judged that he did not. So the difference between Jews and Christians is to be understood in terms of accepting or rejecting the way in which Jesus of Nazareth can be said to be congruent with Israel's expectation, that is, with Israel's language about "He who is to come."

This is the model of messianic ascription that seems to have been operative throughout much of Christian history, and that provided a conceptual base for the sad years of Christian anti-Semitism. There are, in addition, three reasons why this way of understanding the matter is not very fruitful, why it is in fact a dead-end approach. [1] First, the pattern of Jewish expectation in the last centuries before the Common Era was a far more variegated phenomenon than is conventionally and uncritically assumed. To have announced to a first century CE Palestinian Jew that Jesus of Nazareth was the Messiah Come would undoubtedly have elicited the response, "What kind of Messiah?" or "Which Messiah?" The testimony of the canonical gospels certainly is that Jesus' messiahship was not self-evident. That the majority of his fellow-Jews did not acknowledge him as Messiah is clear evidence of that

[2] Second, the title "messiah" [or "Christ"—its Greek equivalent] as it was attached to the name "Jesus" quickly was regarded as part of a proper name, and used interchangeably, so that it became quite commonplace to speak of "Christ" and Jesus" in a variety of combinations. This was more the case as the membership of the Christian assemblies came more and more to be predominantly Gentile. When the majority of believers had no immediate personal connection with the patterns of Jewish expectation, "Jesus Christ" designated the central figure in their religious consciousness, and was understood as a name.[8] The consequence of this was that the tendency to appropriate other titles was accelerated. The proliferation of messianic titles testifies to the need the early Christian generations felt to supplement the simplicity of the use of "messiah."

[3] Third, this way of interpreting the process of messianic ascription seems to be based on the predictive and a-historical use which characterized the early Christian employment of the religious texts inherited from Israel. One need think only, for example, of the Matthean evangelist's appropriation of Hosea 11:1 and Isaiah 7:14 as signs of messianic fulfillment. The churches are well reminded that both the Hosea and Isaiah passages had clear historical and contextual meanings quite different from their early Christian employment.

A variation of this approach that avoids most of these simple-minded errors is suggested by Martin Buber's concern to repatriate Jesus into the authentic heart of Jewish religiousness.[9] In his view, Jesus is our Jewish "brother" who has no cause in or for himself, but speaks and acts only for the cause of God. As such, he is the fulfilled man, although he is not the fulfillment; he is a man of faith, although he is not the object of faith; he is a genuinely messianic man, although he is not the "Messiah Come." "It is a mistake, said Buber, "to regard Jewish Messianism as a belief in an event happening once at the end of time and in a single human figure created as the center of this event."[10] The authentic Jewish vision of redemption is opposed to any sense of the self-differentiation of "one man from other men, of one time from other times, of one act from other actions."[11] Jesus could very well be spoken of as a messianic person under the shadow or model of the servant of God, but Jesus' self-identification [or the churches' identification of him] as "Messiah Come" negated the possibility of his serving a genuinely messianic or servant function for Israel. It is only as a witness who does not call attention to himself, or have such attention called to him, that Jesus can be regarded as a genuine brother to all the sons and daughters of Israel.

A second variation of the conventional and stereotypical approach draws upon the resources of contemporary Jewish scholarship, seeks to acknowledge the wide variety in the patterns of Jewish religiousness in the first century CE, and aims to avoid the theological anachronism of reading the Jewish record in the light of the rabbinic reformulation of Jewish life following the destruction of the Temple in 70 CE. This approach attempts to give a genuinely Jewish reading of the messianic titles. Accordingly, the Johannine language of "the Word made flesh" could be viewed as not being so far removed from Buber's concept of Jesus as "the fulfilled man." The title "Son of God" could be seen as not so far removed from the declaration that the earthly career of the historical Jesus, "the man of faith," is transparent of the divine program for human renewal that the faithful remnant of Israel was called to serve. The "Risen Lord" could be understood as not being so far removed from the messianic confidence that injustice, oppression, and suffering are not the end of the human story. This approach depends for its fruitfulness upon recognizing the ambiguity present in all application of metaphors to the figure of Jesus.

This first approach can be seen also as exemplified in the conciliar definitions of Jesus as "very God of very God," and "very man of very man" [Nicaea], joined together in inseparable unity [Chalcedon]. One could say that this is simply another example of the one-way view of the dynamic of messianic ascription. We have a preliminary idea of what "God," "man," and "unity" mean. In the light of these given definitions and understandings we apply the terms to the figure of Jesus and say of him that he fits or matches the definitions, that he is the hypostatic union of the divine and human. But these terms are as multivalent as the titles inherited from Israel, and the one-way approach is no more helpful here than it was in the Christological reflection of the New Testament period, since it too ignores the ambiguity built into the evaluating situation.

The conventional Christological procedure looked at the figure of Jesus in the light of his capacity to match one or more pictures from the gallery of earlier Jewish anticipation. This interpretation of the religious and theological evaluation in the communities of the New Testament period has traditionally been taken as well to the deliberations of Nicaea and Chalcedon, looking at the figure of Jesus in the light of his capacity to match the models of divinity, humanity, and unity derived from the Neo-Platonic metaphysical vision. For several reasons this perspective on the Christological procedure is of limited value: [1] existing messianic models were too ambiguous to make easy application to the figure of Jesus; [2] the early practice of turning "Jesus the Christ" into the proper name "Jesus Christ" and the corollary use of a multiplicity of terms make it inadvisable to invest too much significance in any one term; [3] an uncritical, almost mechanical, view of prophecy and fulfillment is presupposed. From the point of view of this approach, revisioning Christology is unnecessary and alternative Christologies impossible.

3. MESSIANIC NAMING AS DIALECTICAL

A different Christological procedure avoids these problems by recognizing that this ascriptive process is logically a dialectical one, rather than the one-way dynamic of the traditional mode, and embraces wholeheartedly the inescapable ambiguity such a process entails. This two-way or double dynamic acknowledges that all of the many titles utilized by the New Testament writers and by the shapers of conciliar language had an existence, usage, and history either in Hebraic thought or in classical metaphysics which were prior to their Christian employment. This perspective observes further, however, that each of these honorifics receives new content, new meaning, and new significance when predicated of Jesus, or used as an explanatory model to elucidate the extraordinariness of Jesus. When Christians of these early centuries sought for ways to give conceptual expression to their experience of renewal, empowerment, and commission in relation to Jesus, they drew upon the biblical and philosophical terminology known to them. They did this for two reasons: [1] either because these terms were suggestive and came as close as possible to identifying some salvific aspect of the Jesus experience, or [2] because their usage ruled out some other way of talking that seemed to violate the communities' deepest intuitions and that accordingly seemed outside the parameters of acceptable variety. These considerations account for one direction of the Christological dynamic. There is a counter movement as well. The depth of the salvation Christians experienced in relation to Jesus and the innovatory character of Jesus' activity and teaching seen over-against the conventions of Palestinian Jewish religiousness were of such power that the best interpretive structures available were found wanting, suggestive, and although not inappropriate, were always imprecise and non-exhaustive. Given the historical context, "messiah" language was the best way to point to the power and authority of Jesus, but the very idea of "messiah" was modified by that very process of predication.

The Gospel according to Luke provides a ready example of the ambiguous and dialectical nature of the logic of messianic ascription. The dynamic here informs the whole range of New Testament titular Christology and provides a hermeneutical key for the conciliar discussions as well. At various times in the tumultuous history of Israel sensitive observers talked about the coming of an ideal king who would restore the fortunes of Israel and establish the triumph of God's power in the world, one who would belong to the dynastic line of David. By the second century before the birth of Jesus, this sense of promise and expectation was expressed in "messiah" language. At that time there emerged the idea of the coming of a future anointed agent of God in the Davidic line. But that hope was voiced in other terms, as is well known. Some indeed hoped for a political king; others, however, spoke in terms of a great prophet, a teacher of the Law, a bearer of angelic power, a priest-ruler, as well as a king in the Davidic tradition. Some did not personify their hope at all, but spoke of a coming messianic age or time. This messianic hope, then, took a wide variety of forms in the decades surrounding the life of Jesus of Nazareth, just as Jewish religiousness in Palestine was expressed in a variety of ways.

When Luke seeks to elucidate the meaning and significance for human history of the career of Jesus of Nazareth, he employs the title "Messiah" [Christ," "Anointed One"]. But as Fitzmyer has pointed out[12] there are fourteen such titles or metaphors that Luke used to symbolize the value Jesus came to have for his followers: teacher, judge, righteous one, holy one, leader, Son of David, king, prophet, servant, Son of Man, Son of God, savior, lord, as well as Christ. With the title "Christ," Luke was able to link Jesus into the pattern of anticipation that characterized Jewish religiousness in the last two centuries BCE. With "Lord," which he uses twice as often as "Christ," Luke was able not only to link Jesus with the Jewish tradition, but also to appeal to a more universal audience, since "kyrios" ["lord"] was not only used in the Septuagint to translate YHWH, the Hebrew divine name, it also meant the central divine figure in several of the religious movements of the Mediterranean world.

The connection of the name "Jesus" with these titles, which vary in their emphasis and frequency from one gospel to another, is to be understood as the joining together of the historical with the metaphorical. "Jesus" is a proper name belonging to a concrete historical individual; "Christ" is a title which means an "anointed" agent of God. These two words are joined long before Luke began his literary project, and as is the case in all the third stage of the development of the gospel tradition, Luke has no interest in either term taken by itself. What each term means is known only by its being joined to the other term. Luke comprehends the meaning of the remembered Jesus by investing him with a wide range of honorifics that had, to be sure, some prior usage and familiarity in Palestinian Jewish thought and the wider Hellenistic world, such as "the Christ." What Luke writes about Jesus of Nazareth is chosen because it reflects or supports the belief in Jesus as "the Christ." But Luke's interpretation is a double movement. What Luke means by "the Christ" is to be discovered only in relation to the remembered career of Jesus. For Luke, the meaning of the term "Christ" is not to be seen simply in the history of its earlier usage, but receives special clarity in relation to the concrete figure of Jesus. The new meaning that Luke gives the term derives especially from Jesus' passion—his suffering and execution.

The fact and the manner of Jesus' death created a conceptual problem for first century Christians. Luke attempts to make that problem into part of the answer. As has been noted above, there was a broad range of messianic models present in Palestinian Jewish life that, for all their diversity, pointed to the historical triumph of God's power for Israel, and through Israel, for the world. But none of these messianic models included the possibility of the anointed agent of God being repudiated, rejected, and ignominiously executed. So the early Christians were confronted with the problem of showing how Jesus of Nazareth could be spoken of as a messiah since he had been crucified. Luke's answer is that Jesus is the messiah, not because he fit any of the models inherited from the Jewish religious tradition, but because he transformed them, filled the concepts with new meaning. What triumphs now is not kingly power but vicarious suffering; not power over another, but identification with the other in distress and alienation. The fact that even those closest to Jesus in Luke's story had a hard time grasping this is evidence of how novel the picture of a "suffering messiah" must have been among first century CE Palestinian Jews.[13] Each time in Luke's narrative that Jesus speaks of his impending suffering and how following him will require one to "take up one's cross daily," Luke describes the disciples as not understanding what Jesus said. [See, for example, the dispute about power that follows the Last Supper in Luke 22:27. Also, the episode of the walk to Emmaus in Luke 24:13ff. The risen but unrecognized Jesus asks the men why they are so distraught. They reply that they were upset because their friend Jesus had been executed and they are disappointed because they had hoped he would have been the one to redeem Israel. Jesus responds to them by correcting their understanding of messiahship: "O foolish men! . . . Was it not necessary that the Christ should suffer . . .?"] For Luke, and the communities for which he is writing, Jesus is the messiah only because the concept is redefined and transfused with the power of vicarious suffering.

This dialectical view of the logic of messianic ascription can also help us understand the choice of language at Nicaea and Chalcedon. This language is frequently criticized by many persons who are concerned to develop an appropriate contemporary form for Christological discourse. Such criticism often attacks the notions of divinity, humanity, and unity as abstract, and particularly judges that the concept of humanity employed at Chalcedon is stoicized and a-historical, despite the council's intention to affirm the full humanity of Jesus. The traditional way of thinking about the ascriptive process can undoubtedly uncover the definitions of these three terms that were presupposed in the debates, and we would be better informed about this historical situation. But this approach leads to the same kind of dead-end that characterized the conventional one-way model of New Testament Christology. If the conciliar project were viewed in the light of the dialectical model, we would be able to appropriate its achievement more signifcantly even if we do not share the world-view that was presupposed in its language. Hardy and Ford[14] have reminded us that divinity and humanity need not be seen as competitive categories. We must not only apply "divinity" and "humanity" to Jesus, but also apply "Jesus" to "divinity" and "humanity"; that is to say, the historical Jesus must be seen as contributing to the definitions of "divinity" and "humanity" themselves.[15] Although this double movement may not describe the historical consciousness of the council fathers, our viewing the ascriptive process as dialectical can help us to discern the inner meaning of their endeavors and to have more profit in the enterprise of developing constructive and contemporary alternatives, since it more self-consciously recognizes the ambiguity of the process.

4. REVISIONING THE NAMING PROCESS

A productive revisioning of Christology is possible to the extent that the dialectical process of messianic ascription is recognized and consciously employed. This revisioning is necessary because of the increasing sense of the inadequacies of titular and creedal Christian definition for a culture that no longer shares the mythological cosmology and the metaphysical certitude of the earlier centuries of Christian believing. Demythologizing and dehellenizing may be useful preliminary moves, but they must be accompanied by a careful reading of our own contemporary reality and sensibility.

Although the interpretive structures utilized by New Testament authors are alien to modern consciousness and cannot meaningfully be recovered, the figure of the historical Jesus [his person, teaching, attitudes, and actions] is accessible to a sufficient degree and with sufficient clarity to serve as the criterion for any Christological reconstruction relevant to people who live on this side of Copernicus, Kant, Darwin, Freud, Pasteur, and Einstein; on this side, as well, of Millett and de Beauvoir, Cone and King, Segundo and Boff. Modern voices from Sobrino to Ruether and Schillebeeckx insist that the logic of Christological reflection requires one to begin with the historical Jesus. "If the *end* of Christology is to profess that Jesus is the Christ, its *starting point* is Jesus of history."[16] This judgment then mandates the difficult task of recovering the distinctive features of the career of Jesus of Nazareth. Such an exegetical enterprise seeks to move through cult and kerygma, to that which gave rise to both cult and kerygma. Although it takes the narrative form of the evangelists' work with utmost seriousness, it recognizes that each narrative expression is not in itself necessarily historical. It notes as well[17] that even the narrative-like context in which the Nicene formulation is set misses much of the phenomenality of the historical Jesus.

Nonetheless, it must be pointed out that professing that "Jesus is the Christ" is not synonymous with making the most accurate or appropriate use of Christological titles, metaphors, or honorifics. The end of Christology cannot be equated with finding the most suitable conceptual way to refer to Jesus. Christological effort is not exhausted by the necessary struggle to understand Jesus "as he really was." Sobrino has cautioned us that ". . . the most urgent task of Christology is to reposition the path and course of believers so that their lives can be a continuing, advancing discipleship, a following of Jesus, and hence a process of concrete filiation as his life was."[18] Ruether has reminded us of the necessity to operate with a Christological model that is not simply the most historically correct, but one that can serve the liberating praxis of present Christian existence.[19] This is not unlike Driver's call for an "ethical Christology."[20] To insist on anchoring the Christological titles in the career of the earthly-historical Jesus moves one to center on the experience of liberation, personal and social transformation that preceded and occasioned the Christological ascriptions in terms of the agent. Such a focus on act rather than on agent might at least enable us to be more concerned to hold together act and agent in our exploration of ways in which one might speak appropriately of Jesus' involvement in God's act of deliverance/liberation/redemption. Driver himself rejects the attempt to make the historical Jesus of the New Testament writings a "Christological norm," in part because what God is doing in our present and future takes priority over the events in first century CE Palestine, although the latter may provide clues. But clues are not norms. Thus he calls for the need to reevaluate both the historical and scriptural Jesus. ". . . christological formulation requires freedom from the past in order to generate a freedom in the present for the sake of the future."[21] Such ethical reformulations become manifestly more possible in the light of the dialectical understanding of messianic ascription. We are not just looking for new titles from our own cultural situation that can elucidate the meaning of Jesus in a relevantly similar way to that of the titles in the New Testament and conciliar decrees. In creating new titles ". . . we must remember that it is from the figure of Jesus himself that we know what it means to be . . ."[22] whatever concept or function or title we predicate of Jesus or ascribe to him. This is the charter for relevant Christological reconstruction in our own time. Many suggestions have been advanced in recent years in the reconstructive project; "brother" [Buber], "man for others" [Bonhoeffer], "friend" {Ruether], "the omega point of evolution"[Teilhard de Chardin], "the absolute bearer of salvation" [Rahner], "liberator" [Boff], "Sophia/wisdom" [Schuessler-Fiorenza], "mother" [Bynum]. Each of these suggestions can have a productive future if and only if it is understood in the dialectical way, and their ambiguity acknowledged. Thus we could pursue one or more of them not because we know in advance what being "friend," "mother," and "liberator" means, but because we are willing to see that it is through Jesus, on the basis of the ascription, that we learn what "friend," "mother," and "liberator" really means.[23]. Yet the end of Christology is not conceptual clarity and usefulness; it is rather to become the friend, the mother, the liberator, the neighbor in our own lives. Thus a deliberate employment of the dynamic of the ascriptive process dialectically understood means that Christians, at least those who are engaged in Christological reflection, are called to live in a hermeneutic circle from which there is no escape.

NOTES

1. See, e.g., the important study by Paul M. van Buren, *A Theology of the Jewish-Christian Reality*, Part 1, *Discerning the Way*] San Francisco: Harper & Row, 1980], Part 2, *A Christian Theology of the People Israel* [San Francisco: Harper and Row, 1983], Part 3, *Christ in Context* [San Francisco: Harper and Row, 1988].

2. Alexander Kohanski, "Martin Buber's Approach to Jesus," *Princeton Seminary Bulletin*, Vol. 67, No. 1, Winter 1975, pp. 103–115.

3. Jacob Neusner has suggested a new foundation for Jewish-Christian dialogue: ". . . the only way for a Judaic believer to understand Christianity is *within Judaic* terms, and the only way for a Christian believer to understand Judaism is *within Christian* terms. [Jacob Neusner, "There Has Never Been a Judaeo-Christian Dialogue—But There Can Be One," *CrossCurrents*, Vol. 42, No. 1 {Spring 1992}, p. 15.] Neusner identifies the Christian belief in the Incarnation of God in Jesus Christ and the Jewish belief in Israel as the two critical elements that must be pursued in this new way. Such a true dialogue will draw upon Jewish and Christian resources for understanding what to each dialogue partner would appear to be profoundly alien conceptions.

4. See, for example, John Dominic Crossan, *The Historical Jesus: The Life of a Mediterranean Jewish Peasant* [San Francisco: Harper and Collins, 1992], and John P. Meier, *A Marginal Jew: Rethinking the Historical Jesus*, Vol. 1 [New York: Doubleday, 1991], Vol. 2 [New York: Doubleday, 1994].

5. See, for example, Sallie McFague, *Metaphorical Theology*, and Joseph S. O'Leary, "Overcoming the Nicene Creed," *CrossCurrents* Vol. XXXIV, No. 4, Winter 1984–1985, pp. 405–413.

6. McFague, op. cit., pp. 145–192.

7. O'Leary, p. 411.

8. The transformation of "Christ" from title to name was a factor which seems to have facilitated the ingress and accommodation of Gentiles in the new societies, since it diminished the importance of maintaining connection with the patterns of Jewish conceptuality.

9. See my *Mutuality: The Vision of Martin Buber* [Albany: State University of New York Press, 1985], pp. 69–88.

10. Martin Buber, "Spinoza, Sabbati Zvi, and the Baal-Shem," in *The Origin and Meaning of Hasidism*, ed. and trans. Maurice Friedman [New York: Harper Torchbooks, 1968], p. 107.

11. Buber, op. cit., p. 111.

12. Joseph A. Fitzmyer, S.J., *The Gospel according to Luke*, I-IX [Garden City: Doubleday and Company, 1981], pp. 197–219.

13. Martin Buber has shown how the conception of God as "the God of sufferers" arose out of the depth of Israel's suffering, and suggests that the consequent figure of the "suffering Messiah" may not be so foreign to the traditions of Judaism as most Christian and Jewish commentary has insisted. Martin Buber, *The Prophetic Faith* [New York: Harper Torchbooks, 1960; Macmillan, 1949], p. 234.

14. Daniel W. Hardy and David F. Ford, *Jubilate: Theology in Praise* [London: Darton, Longman and Todd, 1984].

15. Ibid., p. 135.

16. Jon Sobrino, *Christology at the Crossroads* [Maryknoll, NY: Orbis Books, 1978], p. xxi.

17. O'Leary, p. 407.

18. Sobrino, p. 342.

19. Rosemary Radford Ruether, *To Change the World* [New York: Crossroad Publishing Co., 1981].

20. Tom Driver, *Christ in a Changing World: Toward an Ethical Christology* [New York: Harper and Row, 1981].

21. Driver, p. 24.

22. Sobrino, p. 272.

23. I do not here demonstrate how such reciprocal learning would go forward in particular cases, except to note that the dynamic would work according to the example of messianic ascription in *The Gospel according to Luke* as discussed earlier.

Chapter Four

The Friend

In the first chapter[1] I pointed out that of all his traveling companions Jesus seems to have been especially close to two persons—Mary of Magdala [known as Mary Magdalene] and John, one of the sons of Zebedee. My aim here is to rehearse some of the evidence in the gospel narratives for these relationships, and to suggest several ways in which they are important for us. This emerging picture of Jesus and his two special companions can give a new depth to the way the churches and others attend to the figure of Jesus[2], can improve the churches' self-understanding with respect to what it means to be communities of faith, and facilitate the way in which the image of Jesus can function for those who either look to or invoke that image to sponsor and support healthy relationships with one another.

The images that the gospel narratives provide us of Jesus' relationship to Mary of Magdala and John are ambiguous. In this case the ambiguity does not present us with what we called earlier the bright and dark sides of the tradition, but rather presents us with the kind of intimations and clues that good stories often contain, in a way quite different from more discursive prose. Jesus' relationships with Mary and John were quite unusual for a first century CE Palestinian Jewish male who was engaged in a public, itinerant teaching program. This fact alone counts heavily in support of their claim to be firmly fixed in the community's early memories.[3] The narratives of Jesus' relationship with either Mary or John are not likely to be inventions of the evangelists' imagination, since they were a matter of embarrassment, or neglect, for the churches' developing Christological reflection.

1. JESUS OF NAZARETH

Lex orandi lex credendi is the venerable and accurate formulaic representation of the experiential roots, origin, and grounding of Christian theological reflection. Conventionally translated [although the phrase admits of other possibilities], the sentence acknowledges that "the law of praying [worship] establishes [is] the law of believing." That is to say, Christian theology is to be understood as a second order affair, a project of rendering coherent, organized, and intelligible what Christian women and men do in their doxological moments, when they sing, pray, confess, testify, celebrate, baptize, witness. All these activities and others as well, are themselves ejaculatory expressions and pointers to a prior self-defining and self-renewing experience.[4] The historical layers of the gospel, epistolary, and other literature of the New Testament attest to this. For example, in his authentic letters, as well as those written in his name, Paul makes references to or incorporates baptismal [e.g., Galatians 3:28], eucharistic [e.g., I Corinthians 11:23–26], creedal [e.g., Romans 1:2–4], and hymnic [e.g., Philippians 2:5–11] fragments from the liturgical activities of the church communities known to him. Thus Paul's theological explorations follow from, depend upon, and explicate the content of word and act of the churches' worshipping life. Also, the gospel narratives, as is well known, are to be understood as the creative weaving together of individual units that had a prior life in or were designed to serve the several needs of the Christian assemblies, one of which was the churches' developing liturgical life. But the act of worship from which this literature takes its rise and is formed to serve, itself depends upon a prior experience, an awareness by men and women of having received a gift of meaning so profound, so unaccountable and gratuitous that they could ascribe its nature and source only to a transcendent power, certainly not to their own talents or natural endowments. The possible states which might be represented by such a "gift of meaning" would include, but not be exhausted by, the sense of being liberated from having one's life situation determined by one's past mistakes, being empowered to act neighborly without conditions or expecting compensation, being sustained in the effort to keep on keeping on. The constant ingredient in these experiences is the sense of contingency, the awareness of being generously attended to by another. The evangelists frequently speak of the disciples as being "utterly astounded" [e.g., Mark 6:51]. Paul asks "What have you that you did not receive?" [I Corinthians 4:7] And the Johannine author acknowledged, "In this is love, not that we loved God but that he loved us." [I John 4:7][5]

Women and men who experienced this giftedness in the context of an encounter with Jesus of Nazareth began to employ interpretive titles or honorifics when naming Jesus that had the extraordinary valence of an earlier use with respect to God.[6] In later reflective periods people began to think through the implications of this reverential mode of speaking, and the tradition's Christological project got under way. The central intellectual problem was always how to hold together both monotheistic conviction and the recognition or belief that God was so peculiarly involved in the career of Jesus that those who came under his purview found themselves reborn, so to speak, an experience of giftedness so overpowering that they could attribute it only to God. The interpretive strategies they pursued to address this problem found them using the metaphors of exaltation, adoption, conception, and pre-existence, leading up to the fourth century Trinitarian definitions. Jesus now could be said to be "the Son of God" because he was "God the Son." This development climaxed with Anselm's classic expression of *Deus Homo [God Man]*, that was not so much a Christological title as it was the recognition that the limits of language had been reached and found to be inadequate. Nonetheless, the intent of all the churches' application of God language to Jesus of Nazareth was always to preserve and to explicate what it meant to say that Jesus of Nazareth was a man, meeting whom gave the highest meaning to human life. Yet the more exalted the language became, the more difficult it was for the churches to hold onto the full significance of its root acknowledgement that Jesus, whatever else he was or may be said to be, was a man—a first century CE Palestinian Jewish male.

The theological task is always how to speak of the "divine" and the "human" as cohering in or as aspects of this one event. The churches used various explanatory models that themselves presupposed various understandings of what it means to speak of "God" and "man," or of the "divine " and the "human."[7] Theological effort was expended in various ways on one or the other side of this duality during the course of Christian history. Despite the frequent imbalance, however, the churches' intention always was to safeguard both dimensions in their fullness and authenticity.

In this effort, safeguarding the humanity of Jesus became the more problematic. Despite the continuing affirmation that Jesus was fully human, councils and commentators often seem to suggest that something happened to Jesus' humanity when juxtaposed with the divine. Two related features of Jesus' humanity have given the churches the most difficulty: Jesus' racial or ethnic particularity [he was a Jew] and Jesus' sexuality [he was a male]. [1] As the population of the Christian assemblies became increasingly Gentile, the relevance and necessity of Jesus' Jewishness seemed to diminish. "Christ," ["Messiah"], originally a Jewish title, soon functioned as a proper name in those communities whose Jewish membership was minimal, or non-existent, a shift which both symbolized and facilitated the transformation of the early

Jesus movement into a trans-racial and trans-national reality; for as a name rather than a title, its meanings in Jewish history would not have to be known or remembered. It is, further, of utmost significance that all of the surviving Christian literature of the first century CE was originally written in Greek.[8] This downplaying of Jesus' Jewishness is suggested, among other ways, by the convention of reading back into the literary presentations of Jesus and his time the polemical controversies between church communities and synagogues that developed in some places toward the end of the first century CE.[9] It reached a crisis formulation in Marcion's mid-second century project to create a Christian canon expunged of all references to and connections with the Hebrew Scriptures. The main-stream Christian communities rejected Marcion's canon on the basis of their intuition that the God they believed to be disclosed in the life of Jesus is the same God disclosed in the life of Israel, and that it was a false lead to suppose that redemption and creation required different groundings. Their formal retention of ties to the texts of the Jewish religious tradition did not, unfortunately, prevent the churches from adopting destructive anti-Semitic attitudes and practices, in which any distinction between the ethnic and religious dimensions of Jewish identity was lost. A final and bizarre form in which this discomfort with Jesus' Jewishness was expressed is the "discovery" of the "German Christians" in the Nazi era, that Jesus was not Jewish at all, but Aryan.[10] A slightly different form of anti-Semitism appeared in the "message Christology"[11] of liberal Protestantism of the 20th century. This religious movement tended to focus on the content of Jesus' teachings as definitive of the Christian vision, and characteristically emphasized those more inclusive, less culture-specific counsels he is described as giving. The consequence of such an emphasis was a tendency to regard Jesus almost as the first "Christian," whose Jewishness, while not denied, was trivialized. All significant contemporary Christological discussion, however, wants to build with full seriousness on the full implication of the undiminished Jewishness of Jesus.[12]

[2] The same cannot be said for the other, related dimension of Jesus' humanity, namely, his sexuality. The churches officially rejected Marcion's deracinating program, and appended a collection of Christian writings to the inherited synagogue texts.[13] But a covert Marcionism has continued to plague the churches' consciousness in different ways across the centuries. In the same way, the churches officially rejected Gnostic and other images of Christ in which some aspect of his humanity was absent, or qualified, and defined his reality in the ecumenical creeds as "Perfect God and Perfect Man."[14] But an even less covert docetism[15] continues to dominate much Christian piety and discourse. Many persons affirm the humanity of Jesus in principle, but are not comfortable with the clear implications of such an affirmation with re-

spect to Jesus' sexuality. But to say that Jesus was fully human means necessarily to say that Jesus was a sexual being. There is no other way to be human, for, as Beverly Wildung Harrison has reminded us, it is human sexuality that "deepens and shapes our power of personal being."[16] Tom Driver has
put it bluntly and correctly: ". . . a sexless Jesus can hardly be conceived to
be fully human."[17]

To talk, then, about Jesus' sexuality is simply to speak in a focused way of
the historical Jesus as being a fully human being. It is not to say anything at
all about Jesus' sexual activity. About that the New Testament is completely
silent. All comment or surmise about how Jesus dealt with and expressed his
sexuality must avoid claiming to know what the sources available simply do
not tell us. The silence of the sources does not, of course, support the sexo-
phobic view that Jesus was somehow sexless. The silence on this and many
other aspects of Jesus' personal life is simply a feature of the common characteristic of the gospel texts for which historical or biographical interest was
never primary.[18] So we do not know whether or not Jesus was ever married,
was sexually active with anyone, male or female. And the picture of Jesus in
the gospels is just that, a picture, that is, whatever historical information the
evangelists do convey is always in service to a theological intention or
agenda. Thus, the Jesus whom we encounter in the gospel narratives is always
a faith-image, or a perspectival image. Consequently, the subject of our inquiry is never Jesus-as-we-are-sure-he-was, but always Jesus-as-he-was-
pictured-to-be.

These limitations do not, however, leave us completely ignorant. As
William E. Phipps has reminded us, the "unanimous conviction of New Testament writers" was "that Jesus was a real Jewish man."[19] Although Phipps is
quite aware of the possibilities and the limitations of the argument from silence, he is surely correct to observe that in a most general way the evangelists' biographical silence "with respect to a prevailing culture should be interpreted to mean that the individual concerned followed the normal pattern
of conduct."[20] Phipps concludes from that observation to the likelihood of Jesus having been married. Such a possibility clearly accords with the cultural
expectations of Jewish life. We do learn that Jesus' brothers were married, as
were most of his apostles, and so we could easily expect the evangelists to
drop some hint that Jesus was or had once been married if that were the case.
Their silence does seem to diminish the likelihood that the cultural norm was
observed in Jesus' case.[21] But, in addition to an awareness of first century CE
Palestinian Jewish practices, we do know a great deal about normal male psychological and physiological development. That leads us to be able to affirm
confidently that being a Jewish male, Jesus had a penis, was circumcised, had
erotic interests and desires, and had erections. What any or all of this meant

to a Jewish boy growing up with brothers and sisters in an observant household, we do not know. The anonymous author of the *Letter to the Hebrews* acknowledges without hesitation that Jesus' humanity clearly meant, among other things, that "in every respect" he "has been tempted as we are, yet without sinning." [Hebrews 4:15] The New Testament, as Phipps correctly observes, "assumes that Jesus had normal sexuality and sexual desire, both of which are essential for humanness . . ."[22] If Jesus' Jewishness was authentic, he could not have regarded sexual desire as immoral. Regarding erotic impulse as evil or sinful in itself would have been characteristic of some strains of Greek thought,[23] not Jewish. What one does with one's sexuality, that is, the conduct of one's sexual life, is properly subject to ethical scrutiny, not the fact of sexuality and the desires or impulses that this engenders. This judgment seems to accord fully with what little the gospels do suggest that Jesus had to say about human sexuality. Hypocrisy, particularly when cloaked with the garb of religion, was far more distressing to him than sexual misadventure.[24] Sexuality is not that from which one needs to be redeemed. On the other hand, contra the fictional imagination of both D. H. Lawrence[25] and Nikos Kazantzakis[26], nowhere does Jesus suggest by word or act that phallic energy or expression is a means of spiritual regeneration. As Driver puts it, we need to insist that the Jesus of the gospels is not "isolated from sexuality, even in his own person," but also is one who has refused "to sanction its religious status."[27]

2. MARY OF MAGDALA

We move now to consider those persons with whom Jesus appears to have had, or at least is pictured as having, especially close affectional relationships. Nothing in what follows is intended to claim any knowledge or to speculate in any way whatever about Jesus' possible sexual activity with any persons. This discussion wants to take seriously, however, the New Testament evidence with respect to Jesus' personal relationships that is often over-looked or insufficiently attended to.

Jesus valued his privacy, often needing to protect his own time and space. But he was not a "loner." He enjoyed parties and other social occasions, and not always as the center of attention. The companions with whom he traveled or with whom he spent time were not always learners or disciples, subservient to and orbiting the master teacher. With some of them Jesus seemed to have enjoyed a high degree of mutuality. Some kinds of piety might be uncomfortable with the suggestion that the man who is said to have loved everybody might have loved some particular persons in a special way, and that such an affection might have been reciprocal. This never appeared to the New Testament writers as inconsistent, however, and, although the display of such deep regard might have been unusual for a Palestinian Jewish male, it seems to have been so firmly rooted in the tradition and in the communities' memories that the writers could not ignore it. What they do tell us is that Jesus' personal life was completely human and normal, that his eros could be expressed in an open, non-possessive way, and that sexuality for him accords with the contemporary understanding of an innate impulse or drive, whose central dynamic is not orgasmic but relational. On this basis we are to understand the loving relationships Jesus is mentioned as having with five persons: Martha, Mary, and their brother Lazarus of Bethany; Mary of Magdala, and John, the son of Zebedee. The evangelist says explicitly that Jesus loved the family from Bethany[28] and John.[29] No writer, however, uses either verb "to love" [*agapao* or *phileo*][30] to characterize Jesus' attitude toward Mary Magdalene. That she was loved by Jesus is an inference drawn from the narratives of their involvement, in which a certain ambiguity is always present. Of these five persons, Mary Magdalene and John are of special interest in this chapter, for the intimacy in these relationships is especially noteworthy.

Jesus' relationship with Mary of Magdala is a special instance of the open, accepting, non-exploitative, and non-patriarchal attitude toward women which the evangelists discern in, report, or attribute to Jesus. This sexually egalitarian attitude is expressed both in the form and content of Jesus' teaching as well as his public actions. To name only a few examples: Jesus publicly associates and travels with women; his work is supported by women; he is instructed by women [Mark 7:24–30], and teaches them; rejects sexual stereotypes [John 8:2–11, Luke 10:38–42], and is an advocate of women who have been oppressed by the economic and religious system of the day. [Mark 12:40; Luke 18:2–5][31] This view is commonly accepted by all current New Testament scholarship, although its significance is variously assessed. Leonard Swidler holds that Jesus was a "feminist," by which he means that a constitutive part of the gospel is the "personalism" which Jesus extended to women.[32] Other commentators, operating from either a general or specific political definition of "feminism," prefer not to speak of Jesus as a feminist as such. While acknowledging Jesus' receptive attitude toward women, Michael Grant believes that this "was not primarily based on either sexual feelings or feminist principles. It was, as always, a logical deduction from his preoccupation with the Kingdom of God: "Why treat women any less favourably than men?"[33] Daphne Hampson, however, rejects the idea that Jesus' attitude toward women was so very exceptional.[34] He certainly did not make "a feminist analysis of society," an historical impossibility in the first century CE. Nonetheless, the evangelists do present a convincing picture of Jesus as "a young, unmarried man—allowing himself to be fondled and kissed by such women,[35] without either embarrassment or acquiescence in their morals. . . . Jesus simply accepts these women as persons . . ."[36]

That Mary Magdalene is a primary figure in the gospel narratives is apparent to any careful reader. She is always named first when several women associates of Jesus are identified. She is an independent woman without any male sponsor [father, husband, brother, uncle], whom Jesus delivered from great distress ["seven demons" {Luke 8:2}]. There is no necessary reason, contra much older commentary, to identify her with the unnamed sinner of Luke 7:36–50. She is the first to see the risen Jesus,[37] and in reporting the experience becomes an apostle to the apostles. John Alsup has convincingly shown that the Magdalene appearance stories are one of four forms of appearance stories that together are an "independent stream of tradition,"[38] that is to say, they are early and firmly fixed in the narrative history.

We are not especially concerned here, however, simply with the primary position as such accorded the Magdalene, but rather with the one narrative in which there is an adumbration of her affectional relationship with Jesus. The appropriateness of interpreting the Johannine appearance pericope in this manner is supported, although not of course confirmed, by the development of the Magdalene tradition in second century gnostic texts.[39] In *The Gospel of Mary* there is reference to a kissing relationship, and *The Gospel of Philip* apparently presents Mary as Jesus' wife. These Nag Hammadi texts not only suggest the apostolic role of Mary Magdalene, but also make explicit the intimacy of the relationship between Jesus and Mary:[40]

> There were three who always walked with the Lord:
> Mary his mother, and her sister and Magdalene, the
> one who was called his companion.
>
> And the companion of the [Savior is] Mary Magdalene.
> [But Christ loved] her more than [all] the disciples
> [and used to] kiss her [often] on her mouth.[41]
>
> Peter said to Mary, "Sister, we know that the Savior
> loved you more than the rest of the women."[42]
>
> Levi said, ". . . Surely the Savior knows her very well.
> That is why he loved her more than us."[43]

The scholarly consensus is that although these texts do not come from communities that were part of the developing "Great Church,"[44] they do reveal the fact that some Christian assemblies in this early period were accustomed to picturing the relationship between Jesus and Mary in such an affectional manner. There is no reason to regard this as anything but a natural development of the images in the Synoptic and Johannine traditions. Further, since "Christ loved her more than all the other disciples" is a close parallel to "the disciple whom Jesus loved more than all the other disciples," and since the latter, according to Hans-Martin Schenke, is the equivalent of "the disciple whom Jesus loved," Mary Magdalene may even have been the figure on the basis of which the Johannine redactor modeled "the Beloved Disciple."

We shall confine ourselves, nonetheless, to the Johannine text, in which there is, as Grant cautions,[45] no justification for supposing that Mary Magdalene was Jesus' mistress, although, as we will suggest, every reason to see her pictured here as a "special friend"[46] of Jesus. Since the present form of the appearance narrative in John 20:1–18 is a conflation of two pericopes [the Mary pericope in verses 1, 11–18, and the Peter/Beloved Disciple pericope in 3–10, with verse 2 being a transition device][47] we will separate out the Magdalene appearance narrative as the text for our commentary.

> {1} Early on the first day of the week, while it was still dark, Mary Magdalene came to the tomb and saw that the stone had been removed from the tomb. . . . {11} Mary stood weeping outside the tomb. As she wept, she bent over to look into the tomb; {12} and she saw two angels in white, sitting where the body of Jesus had been lying, one at the head and the other at the feet. {13} They said to her, "Woman, why are you weeping?" She said to them, "They have taken away my Lord, and I do not know where they have laid him." {14} When she had said this, she turned around and saw Jesus standing there, but she did not know that it was Jesus. {15} Jesus said to her, "Woman, why are you weeping? Whom are you looking for?" Supposing him to be the gardener, she said to him, "Sir, if you have carried him away, tell me where you have laid him, and I will take him away." {16} Jesus said to her, "Mary!" She turned and said to him in Hebrew [that is, Aramaic], "Rabbouni!" [which means Teacher]. {17} Jesus said to her, "Do not hold on to me, because I have not yet ascended to the Father. But go to my brothers and say to them, 'I am ascending to my Father and your Father, to my God and your God.'" {18} Mary Magdalene went and announced to the disciples, "I have seen the Lord'" and she told them that he had said these things to her. [NRSV]

The central features of the appearance to Mary Magdalene are these: early on Sunday morning Mary Magdalene goes to the tomb of Jesus, with no motive identified. She finds the tomb empty, save for the divine messengers who interpret the significance of this to Mary. As she is weeping, the Risen Jesus appears to her, but she does not recognize him, suspecting him to be the gardener who might, quite understandably, have information about the disposition of the body. Jesus engages in conversation with her; and when he speaks to her by name, she recognizes him. Jesus tells her not to hold on to him, and then gives her a message to convey to his other disciples, which she proceeds to do.

Most commentators on this pericope read the passage for the light it might shed on a number of theological issues.[48] This approach is natural and appropriate since the Johannine as well as the Synoptic gospels are theological representations of the event of Jesus as the Christ in narrative form,[49] differing from the intention of the Pauline literature, authentic or pseudonymous, chiefly in the literary genre employed—narrative rather than epistolary. Central among these issues are the following questions: [1] What is suggested here about the relation of the empty tomb to the rise of faith in the Risen Jesus? [2] What is suggested here about the nature of the resurrection itself? [3] What is suggested here about the nature of the Risen Jesus? [4] Finally, what is suggested here about the character of leadership in the early Christian assemblies?

One who reads the pericope carefully with these questions in mind will discover the following: [1] The empty tomb is not in itself productive of faith in the Risen Jesus. It may be confirmatory or illustrative of resurrection faith, functioning, perhaps as "an idiom of Christological insight," like the virginal conception.[50] But it is a datum which must be accounted for. Mary's initial sense was that the body had simply been removed. Since the tomb was located in a garden, her question to the one she mistakenly assumed to be the gardener was perfectly natural. The absence of Jesus' body had to be explained, which must have been the function of the "two angels in white" in the original form of the narrative. The empty tomb, then, takes its place alongside all other signs and clues that the disciples do not understand.

[2] The Mary Magdalene pericope tells us nothing about the resurrection itself, and its silence on this matter, wholly consistent with the Synoptic tradition, needs to be recognized. Although these stories are customarily called "resurrection narratives," they are, in fact, not accounts of the resurrection at all, but are rather appearance narratives. The traditions all agree [which suggests that the sequence was fixed very early in the communities' proclamation], that Jesus of Nazareth was executed by Roman authority on Friday, that he died rather quickly for victims of this form of capital punishment, and was buried. He was really dead! This same Jesus, now risen and transformed, so as to be discernible only with the eyes of faith, appeared to his dispirited disciples on Sunday, and for a short time thereafter. But nowhere in the canonical gospels is their either speculation or a narrative picturing of the resurrection, the event of Jesus' rising or being raised from the dead. Not until the second century Gnostic text *The Gospel of Peter*[51] does the pious imagination reduce the textual silence on this matter by providing an account of the resurrection. The Magdalene story, like the Synoptic accounts, is religiously circumspect on this point, completely devoid of any speculative attempt to extinguish the mystery. This pericope is not, then, a resurrection narrative as

such, but a recognition narrative, whose dynamic is the initiatory movement of the Risen Jesus himself.

[3] There is a clear synonymity between the historical Jesus and the Risen Jesus, between Jesus as he was seen and heard in the hills and villages of the Galilee and Judea, and Jesus as he was discerned, by faith, to be present to gatherings of his friends following his execution. But there is a difference. That the one who confronts Mary is the Risen Jesus is not self-evident, but like the empty tomb, has to be interpreted. That interpretation is provided by the Risen Jesus himself, not so much by way of an explanation, but by another sign or act. In this case, that act is the Risen Jesus' calling to Mary by name. This scene thus recalls the Emmaus pericope in Luke [Luke 24:13–35], in which the Risen Jesus appears to the disciples on their walk to the village, but is not recognized by them until, in Eucharistic fashion, he blesses and shares bread with them: "He was known to them in the breaking of the bread." [Luke 24:35] In both appearance stories the Risen Jesus must do or say something to enable the disciples or Mary to recognize him. The appearances are thus revelatory occasions, productive of religious faith, but not produced by it.

[4] The Mary Magdalene pericope is narrative testimony to the apostolic and kerygmatic authority of women in the Johannine community. The reader has been prepared for this climax by two earlier episodes in which women function in this special, authoritative way. First, the pericope of Jesus and the Samaritan woman [John 4:1–42]. At the beginning the woman regards Jesus only as a traveling Jewish male, sufficiently independent and self-assured as to request a drink of water from her at the well. In the course of the conversation she moves to acknowledge him as a prophet, and finally receives his messianic self-revelation in the formula common to John's Gospel: "I am he, the one who is speaking to you." [v. 26] Jesus self-reference here—"I am"—is the formula of divine self-disclosure in Exodus 3:14, and John uses this in a programmatic fashion when explaining Jesus' nature and mission.[52] The woman leaves the well, goes into the city, and reports her experience to the people, with the result that "Many Samaritans from that city believed in him, because of the woman's testimony." [v. 36] Her difficulty in recognizing Jesus' true identity, what Paul Duke calls "the irony of identity,"[53] and her proclamatory response to Jesus' self-revelation anticipates the recognition and testimony motifs of the Mary Magdalene story.

Second, the pericope of Jesus with Martha and Mary at the time of Lazarus' death [John 11:1–57]. Jesus and those traveling with him have arrived in Bethany after Lazarus has died. Martha goes out to meet Jesus while Mary stays at home. In their conversation Martha at first thinks that Jesus' confidence that Lazarus "will rise again" [v. 28] is a reference to the common

Jewish belief in a general resurrection at the last day. Her confusion is reduced with Jesus' self-predication, again in the characteristic Johannine fashion: "I am the resurrection and the life." [v. 25]; and she finally acknowledges not the truth of the statement ["Do you believe this?"], but the true identity of Jesus: "Yes, Lord, I believe that you are the Christ, the Son of God, the one coming into the world." [v. 27] What John has done here is to have Martha give voice to the Johannine communities' Christological confession,[54] in the same language with which the gospel originally ended: "But these are written that you may come to believe that Jesus is the Christ, the Son of God . . ." [20:31]. This means that Martha now is the voice, not of the unspecified affirmation of the Samaritan woman, but of the creedal affirmation of the church communities.[55]

The reader is thus prepared for Mary Magdalene to be the first to see the risen Jesus; that, according to the author of Acts, is a necessary condition for apostleship [Acts 1:23] She recognizes him, as we have seen, only after her mistaken impressions are corrected by the Risen Jesus' self-revelation as he speaks to her by name. She responds to Jesus' instruction by reporting to the other disciples, saying "I have seen the Lord." [v. 18] Just as Martha spoke with the Christological language of the Johannine community, so Mary here refers to Jesus as "Lord," the primitive Christological confession of the Christian assemblies.[56] This is the first time in John that the title unfailingly applied to the God of Israel is applied to the Risen Jesus.

The woman of Samaria and Martha of Bethany have thus anticipated and foreshadowed the kerygmatic and apostolic function of Mary of Magdala. In this way, the evangelist has carefully provided the sanction for his community's egalitarian praxis.

These are some of the insights that might be gained by reading the Mary Magdalene pericope with a set of explicitly theological questions in mind. But what might be seen in the story if it is read from a different perspective, with, that is, the lens of human affection, the biographical-historical rather than the theological?[57]

I suggest that three features take on a different meaning if one reads the narrative with the expectation that it might intimate or disclose something about Mary's relationship to Jesus. We will attempt to look at the story now through this personal or affectional lens.

[1] Mary goes to the tomb alone, early in the morning while it is still dark, unaccompanied by any of the other women named in the Synoptic versions. There was some danger in such a situation, since Jesus had been executed under warrant as a threat to state security. No motive for her action is suggested, such as anointing the body, or completing the burial arrangements put off by the need for a quick burial on Friday before the Sabbath began. She expresses

no anxiety about needing to have the heavy stone wheeled away from the front of the tomb. She simply goes to the garden tomb and weeps there. A. M. Hunter is one of the very few commentators who makes anything in particular about this, suggesting that she might be going to the tomb to render the last offices of love.[58] But even he draws no further conclusion from his own observation. Yet anyone who has loved deeply can easily understand the dynamic of this part of the pericope: the tears, the risk-taking, the desire simply to be there by the beloved. Three times in this short pericope Mary expresses her distress in almost identical language: "They have taken away . . ." [20:2, 13, 15], a narrative device that accentuates the sense of loss that any person who has loved deeply will understand.[59] Mary does what loving, special friends would do in situations of this sort.

[2] The recognition scene is constituted by personal address. The Risen Jesus asks, "Woman, why are you weeping? Whom are you looking for?" Notice that he does not ask, "*What* are you looking for?" The personal pronoun anticipates the personal meeting, implying that the weeping might have to do with him, not the loss of some object that had been misplaced. His voice does not establish his identity; that is disclosed only when he speaks to her by name, "Mary," an unusual act for a Jewish male and teacher to do. Hearing her name uncovers for her the identity of the mystery. From the theological point of view, one might be led to stress the connection between this personal address and the notice in John 10:3, where the good shepherd calls his sheep by name, and they know him. Viewed with the lens of affection, however, we are led to consider the way personal relationships are occasioned and facilitated by the partners' mutual naming. Mary now realizes that this is not the gardener, but her special friend Jesus. In this emotionally charged scene Mary responds, "Rabbouni." Some scholars see this as a disguised Christological affirmation, since this form is sometimes used of God rather than of a human teacher. Others, however, see this as a form which can be best translated as "My dear master," or "My little master."[60] Seeing it as a term of endearment would be consistent with the fact that "Lord" rather than "rabbi" in one of its variations became the Christological title of choice for the primitive communities.

[3] Mary moves to make physical contact with the Risen Jesus, who then says to her, "Do not hold on to me." Those whose interest is primarily theological judge that Mary here has moved to cling to Jesus' feet in an act of adoration, paralleling Matthew's description of the response of the disciples to whom the Risen Jesus has revealed himself: "And they came up and took hold of his feet and worshiped him." [Matthew 28:9] So John Marsh can comment, "Imagination can picture her clasping the feet of Christ in humble adoration."[61] But a sensuous imagination can also picture her embracing the

Risen Jesus as they may simply have been wont to do for some time. Older criticism tends to read the verb in question, *me mou artou*, in the light of the Vulgate rendering, *Noli me tangere*, "Do not touch me." Most contemporary commentary, however, recognizes that the meaning of the command is for Mary to discontinue a physical act already begun, to put an end to action already in progress.[62] And that action can easily and quite naturally be understood as the personal touch and embrace that close friends might customarily exchange, especially after an absence either of length or intensity.[63]

My claim throughout this discussion is not that the pericope necessarily and only means or requires that Mary and Jesus had a relationship of touching intimacy, that their relationship was characterized by mutual love. My point is simply that the story is ambiguous, and that this ambiguity not only admits but can well be illuminated by the supposition of this special friendship. Indeed, the relationship adumbrated by these three moments in the story is a natural expression of the normal erotic dimension of Jesus' humanity. Mary is not the object of Jesus' regard because she had been victimized by the inherited structures of society; she is not befriended as a type, but loved as a person. "Jesus said to her, 'Mary?' She turned and said to him, 'Rabbouni.'"

3. JOHN, SON OF ZEBEDEE

A central, but anonymous figure in the Fourth Gospel is a disciple referred to as the man whom Jesus loved. We examine here the six references to this so-called "Beloved Disciple"[64] with a view to seeing what they might suggest about the character of Jesus' affectional relationships. The reader is advised to recall the parameters set by the texts for a consideration of Jesus' sexuality. As was the case in our earlier discussion of Mary of Magdala, we here make no proposals, nor could we ever achieve any certitude with respect to a knowledge of Jesus' sexual activity. The narratives are too ambiguous for that. But their being ambiguous means also that some data are provided which fall into place and gain new intelligibility if one were to extrapolate from the initial recognition of Jesus as a fully sexual being to make normal conjecture about the special bond that existed between Jesus and this unnamed young man. Jesus' eros was clearly expressed in an intimate, touching involvement with these two special companions—Mary Magdalene, and the Beloved Disciple. That there was any other kind of sexual expression, although certainly plausible, we cannot say or even surmise with any degree of probability. Most commentary avoids speculation altogether on the sexual subtext of these narratives. The result of such silence or avoidance is a strangely artificial picture of Jesus, in which his humanity, while affirmed, is not celebrated in as fully orbed a way as the texts permit and as Christian faith requires.

This special disciple appears in six passages. In all but the last, Jesus is said explicitly to have "loved" him; *agapan* is used in all of these except John 20:2–10, where the verb is *philein*. I have emphasized those phrases in the texts that will be especially significant for our analysis.

1. At the Last Supper [13:23–26]

One of his disciples—*the one whom Jesus loved—was reclining next to him.* Simon Peter therefore motioned to him to ask Jesus of whom he was speaking. So *while reclining next to Jesus*, he asked him, "Lord, who is it?" Jesus answered, "It is the one to whom I give this piece of bread when I have dipped it in the dish."

2. At the Cross [19:25–27]

Meanwhile, standing near the cross of Jesus were his mother, and his mother's sister, Mary the wife of Clopas, and Mary Magdalene. When Jesus saw his mother and *the disciple whom he loved* standing beside her, he said to his mother, "Woman, here is your son." Then he said to the disciple, "Here is your mother." And from that hour the disciple took her into his own home.

3. Outruns Peter [20:2–10]

So she ran and went to Simon Peter and the other disciple, *the one whom Jesus loved*, and said to them, "They have taken the Lord out of the tomb, and we do not know where they have laid him." Then Peter and the other disciple set out and went toward the tomb. The two were running together, but the other disciple outran Peter and reached the tomb first. He bent down to look in and saw the linen wrappings lying there, but he did not go in. Then Simon Peter came, following him, and went into the tomb. He saw the linen wrappings lying there, and the cloth that had been on Jesus' head, not lying with the linen wrappings but rolled up in a place by itself. Then the other disciple, who reached the tomb first, also went in, and he saw and believed; for as yet they did not understand the scripture, that he must rise from the dead. Then the disciples returned to their homes.

4. In the fishing boat with Peter [21:7]

That disciple whom Jesus loved said to Peter, "It is the Lord!"

5. Seen by Peter [21:20–23]

Peter turned and saw *the disciple whom Jesus loved* following them; *he was the one who had reclined next to Jesus at the supper* and said, "Lord, who is it that is going to betray you?" When Peter saw him, he said to Jesus, "Lord, what about him?" Jesus said to him, "If it is my will that he remain until I come, what is that to you? Follow me!"

6. Witness for the gospel tradition [21:24]

This is the disciple who is testifying to these things and has written them, and we know that his testimony is true.

Most commentators examine these passages for the light they may shed on a number of textual and theological issues. As we observed with respect to the Mary Magdalene pericope, such an approach is natural and appropriate, given the theological nature of the text. This is particularly so in the Fourth Gospel. Its redaction history is more complicated, and thus more interesting to some scholars, perhaps, than that of the Synoptics. It discloses a different and probably later perspectival image of Jesus, and provides a window for seeing how broad was the range of possibilities that the Christian assemblies were pursuing toward the end of the first century. Central among these issues are the following questions: [1] Does the language of "Beloved Disciple" point to an historical person or to a type of discipleship? [2] If it refers to a person, who is it most likely to have been? [3] If it refers to a type, what sort of discipleship model is suggested, and what view of the church community is implied by this model? We will not pursue in detail the evidence relevant to an adjudication of these questions, but it will be useful at least to sketch the story in order to show that when the texts are read with these questions in mind, they are found to be productive of important insights and puzzles, such as the following:

> [1] Finally, John recognizing that the bodily facts had been treated in the [Synoptic] gospels, . . . inspired by the Spirit, wrote a "spiritual gospel." [Clement of Alexandria][65]

Clement [c. 150–2115] was apparently alluding to the pervasive use of symbols by the Johannine author. Although all modern discussion of John's gospel rejects Clement's way of contrasting the Fourth Gospel and the Synoptics [as if one gives interpretation and the others biography], it recognizes that a developed interest in symbolic significance is a distinguishing characteristic of the Fourth Gospel.[66] We should not be surprised, then, that many biblical interpreters see in the Beloved Disciple a symbol, a type, or a model, rather than an historical figure. Bultmann judges that "it is not his person, but what he stands for that is represented by the beloved disciple,"[67] and A. Kragerud goes even further to claim that the Beloved Disciple is "purely and simply a fiction."[68]

Apart from a general tendency to downplay the historicity of the Johannine tradition, there appear to be two features of the way the Beloved Disciple is described in the narratives that lead some commentators to believe that he is a type, not an historical person. *First*, he is never named. In none of the six references is his anonymity reduced. This is a principal and telling consideration for Bultmann. Yet, it can hardly be decisive evidence against his historicity. Jesus' mother is never named in the Fourth Gospel, yet no one has ever suggested that, for all her symbolic value, she was not an historical person in her own right. *Second*, some of the terminology, particularly in Greek, seems so symbolic that it is hard not to suppose the author's intention is to portray this person as "the type of true discipleship."[69] For example, John is said to be "beloved" [*agapetos*] of Jesus, just as Jesus is said to be "beloved" [*agapetos*] of the Father. Hoskyns puts it this way: "As Jesus is in the bosom of the Father, so the Beloved Disciple lies in the bosom of the Son."[70] But Hoskyns means by this only that the perfect relationship of disciples to Jesus is anticipated historically in the relation of the Beloved Disciple to Jesus. Grundmann speaks in a similar way: "The place at Jesus' side corresponds to the place of Jesus at the Father's side, just as this place makes him the revealer of the Father, so the beloved disciple's place makes him Jesus' revealer and exegete."[71] Thus, he is the "archetype of a discipleship which makes bearers of revelation out of hearers of revelation."[72]

Now there is no doubt that the Beloved Disciple is portrayed in an idealized fashion, and that he has special symbolic significance in the narrative, as does much in the Fourth Gospel. There is no necessary contradiction, however, between his being a genuine historical figure, and his serving in an idealized capacity for this imaginative and perceptive author. Accordingly, the majority of scholars agree with Mussner and Brown that one need not choose between the Beloved Disciple's being person or type. "The Disciple was idealized, of course," Brown writes, "but in my judgment the fact that he was a historical person and companion of Jesus becomes all the more obvious in the new approaches to Johannine ecclesiology."[73] Thus, "John does not present the Disciple as a pure symbol without historical reality."[74]

[2] If, in Brown's words, "the recognition of the secondary symbolic dimension of the Beloved Disciple" does not obviate "the quest for his identity,"[75] who are the possible candidates in the text, and which is most probable? Several persons, from time to time, have been considered to be the historical figure in the gospel story spoken of as the Beloved Disciple.[76] But

the only persons who have received serious and more than occasional consideration are Mary Magdalene, Martha, Lazarus, and John, the Son of Zebedee. The criteria that the person would have to meet would seem to include the following: [a] some evidence by word and/or deed, preferably by word in this case, that Jesus did indeed love this person in a special way; [b] some evidence that this person was a disciple and closely enough identified with Jesus to have been believably included among those present at the supper; [c] some evidence that this person could have been a witness to or a source of some of the traditions and memories utilized by the Johannine circle in the production of the gospel text.

Now how do the persons named above stand in relation to these criteria? Mary Magdalene, Martha and Lazarus meet the first criterion, although the Johannine author never says that Jesus loved Mary. That is an inference we have drawn from the way in which her relationship to Jesus is described But the author does say that Jesus loved Martha and her brother Lazarus [11:5]. Jesus seems to have been a familiar in their home in Bethany, where he customarily visited when his travels took him to Judea. They were obviously close friends. Further, Lazarus' death was a cause of great sorrow for Jesus [11:35], and as we noted earlier in this chapter, Martha gives voice [11:27] to the gospel's high Christological affirmation repeated at the original ending of the book [20:30–31]. Yet the author never suggests that either Martha or Lazarus was a member of the company of women and men who traveled with Jesus, and this would seem to be a very important consideration. Mary Magdalene, on the other hand, was in that company. All three could have been present at Jesus' farewell supper, but of none of them is there any tradition of having lived long enough to have become the witness to the community at Ephesus' memories, as is presupposed in the epilogue [21:24].[77] Whoever it was, his or her relationship with Jesus must have been so special and so public as to have come to be known by the community as "a specially intimate disciple,"[78] as "the disciple whom Jesus loved." As Bacon reminds us, this is a "title of extreme and exclusive honor."[79]

John, the Son of Zebedee, did not, of course, write the Fourth Gospel, but the early tradition of his residence in Ephesus makes it quite plausible that he lived to such an age as to have been the witness, perhaps indirect, to the traditions which surfaced in the evangelist's revisionist project. He was one of the Twelve, traveling regularly with Jesus, and was, in fact, part of the inner trio of that group [Peter, James, and John]. The general scholarly consensus is that on the basis of these factors [regular association with Jesus, residence in Ephesus, the tradition of "authorship"], and in the absence of any convincing contrary indications, John the son of Zebedee is the most likely person to have become known as the Beloved Disciple, and thus very

likely to have been the man whom Jesus loved. [80] We may never know for
sure, but the absence of even any reasonable certitude on this matter will
have no bearing on our inquiry into what the textual references to the
Beloved Disciple imply about Jesus' affectional relationships. The narratives
may be less intelligible if the Beloved Disciple were not an historical figure;
but the significance of the picture of the Beloved Disciple for the Johannine
perspectival image of Jesus, and the importance of that faith image for the
humanization of contemporary life in no way depend on the Beloved Disciple's ordinary historicity.

[3] Those who are inclined to see the Beloved Disciple as a type rather than
pursue an inquiry into his possible historical identity tend to refer to him by
title—"the Beloved Disciple." This preference is more determinative for their
commentaries than might, at first glance, seem to be the case. By stressing the
title one avoids speaking of "the one whom Jesus loved," and focuses instead
on his being a special kind of disciple. That habit, in turn, then directs attention to the nature of the discipleship that is being symbolized rather than what
is being suggested about this expression of Jesus' eros.

For Hunter, the discipleship appears to be one of apprenticeship or learning,
and the relationship of the Beloved Disciple to Jesus becomes the proper subor-
dination of student to teacher. Hunter accordingly offers "his Master's favourite
pupil"[81] as an appropriate alternative to "Beloved Disciple." Such an approach,
however, does not seem consistent with the kind of intimacy, the degree of mutuality in the relationship that the narratives imply. The Beloved Disciple, as
Brown understands him, "is as intimate with Jesus as Jesus is with the Father."[82]

Bultmann concludes that the Beloved Disciple represents Gentile Christianity,[83] not, of course, in an ethnic sense, but "in so far as it is the authentic
Christendom [sic] which has received its own true self-understanding,"[84] that
is to say, a form of Christian faith which has liberated itself from all ties to
Jewish self-understanding. The contrast is with Mary, Jesus' mother, who in
his view, on the basis of her loyalty at the cross represents Jewish Christianity, and with Peter, over against whom the Beloved Disciple has superiority.
[At the supper, e.g., Peter must ask the Beloved Disciple to ask Jesus who the
betrayer is.] Few have followed Bultmann here, in seeing a contrast between
Mary and the Beloved Disciple. Further, while recognizing a certain tension
between Peter and the Beloved Disciple in the Fourth Gospel, most scholars
tend not to see the Johannine Jesus rejecting the former in favor of the latter.
It puts far too much strain on the text to think that it is evidence for a Johannine countermove to the Petrine claims of the Roman See.

Elisabeth Schuessler-Fiorenza[85] and Raymond Brown[86] both recognize that
the kind of discipleship symbolized by the Beloved Disciple depends very
much on taking very seriously the fact that this disciple is *beloved*, loved by

Jesus in a special way or to a special degree, and that this kind of discipleship has an immediate implication for the nature of the Christian community. For Brown, the Johannine model antedates the concentration of attention on the Twelve. While not opposing the need for authority and order in the church, this model stresses a shared closeness to Jesus as the common, unifying quality of church life. The willingness of the later network of churches to include the Fourth Gospel in its canon should be understood as a willingness to live with the tension between necessarily having structures of authority in the churches, and regarding one another as equally called by and dependent upon a live connection to Jesus.[87]

Elisabeth Schuessler-Fiorenza carries Brown's point a bit further. Her interpretation does not depend upon her view that Martha is a "beloved disciple," but is certainly nourished by this way of reading the narratives. The kind of discipleship symbolized and sponsored by the Beloved Disciple is not only a community of equals, in which the authority of the Twelve is not yet stressed. The Beloved Disciple is the apostolic authority and symbolic center for a church community that is "constituted as the discipleship of equals by the love they have for one another."[88] She thus finds the Beloved Disciple to be the warrant and charter for understanding the church as "a community of friends,"[89] a picture which the Fourth Gospel suggests goes back to Jesus himself, who said, "I do not call you servants any longer, . . . but I have called you friends." [John 15:15].[90]

These are some of the insights that might be gained by attending to the Beloved Disciple references with a set of explicitly theological questions in mind. But what might be seen if these passages are attended to from a different perspective, with, that is, the lens of human affection, rather than the theological?

I suggest that one pericope in particular takes on a different meaning if one reads the narrative with the expectation that it might intimate or disclose something about John's relationship to Jesus. We will attempt to look at part of the Johannine narrative of the Last Supper now through this personal or affectional lens.

> One of his disciples—the one whom Jesus loved - was reclining next to him. Simon Peter therefore motioned to him to ask Jesus of whom he was speaking. So while reclining next to Jesus, he asked him, "Lord, who is it?" Jesus answered, "It is the one to whom I give this piece of bread when I have dipped it in the dish." [John 13:23–26]

The important thing to notice here is not just the designation of this disciple as the one "whom Jesus loved," a naming that occurs, as we have seen, in five passages. The Last Supper pericope provides some content to that love. No reader can miss the author's acknowledgement of a special relationship here, but commentators tend to ask what it tells us in general about discipleship in the Fourth Gospel. We shall ask what it might tell us, in particular, about Jesus' friendship with John, and will look at the character of that friendship as it is identified, not just in naming him as "the disciple whom Jesus loved," but as it is suggested in the seating arrangements and body posture at the Last Supper.

The text does not tell us very much about the kind of table, body posture, or seating arrangements at the Last Supper, except that John was next to Jesus and that Peter was close enough to John to be within ear-shot. The cultural context, however, provides a number of clues, on the basis of which we can infer the following picture. The thirteen men were not sitting at a table, but were reclining, not sitting, on the floor, which would have been the Roman custom. The reclining position at meals is presumed in Luke 7:38 as well as the Fourth Gospel narrative. Although the Johannine chronology makes it doubtful that the Last Supper was a Passover seder as such, it seems to have been Passover-like, and as Marsh indicates, "It was the Passover that was eaten in the reclining position."[91] The usual procedure was to recline sideways, propped up on the left elbow to support the body, with the right arm thus free for use.[92] The position of honor would be to the left of Jesus, the host, while a trusted friend would be to the right of the host.[93] Thus, John would be reclining on Jesus' right with his head close to Jesus' breast. "He was consequently able to hold easy and quite intimate conversation with Jesus."[94] Peter was apparently not so placed that he could ask his question himself, although the natural place for him would have been at Jesus' left side. There is no necessary contradiction in having Peter so located and his still deferring to John to ask Jesus about the betrayer's identity since, as Schenke suggests, most of the references to the Beloved Disciple [except at the cross][95] function to show the superiority of the Beloved Disciple to Peter.[96]

John is pictured thus as reclining next to Jesus, leaning back on his breast, and Jesus' right arm could then quite naturally be around John, embracing him from time to time during the meal, a gesture not stated explicitly but certainly consistent with and probably presumed in the text.

The bodily expression of this male friendship image is absent from the familiar Renaissance representation of the Last Supper that has informed so much of western consciousness—Leonardo da Vinci's painting on the refectory wall of Sante Maria delle Grazie in Milan.[97] Leonardo does not place any of the disciples close to Jesus. Although Jesus' hands are extended out toward the bread and wine in a eucharistic gesture, Leonardo's main concern is not sacramental, but portraying the reaction of the disciples to Jesus' announcement of his impending betrayal. Other artists were able to portray John and Jesus touching, but in ways that did not deflect from their primary emphasis, whether it was eucharistic, reaction to the betrayal announcement, a non-sacramental meal, or founding the community on the basis of the Johannine commandment and enacted parable of mutual love. Yet artistic representation of the Last Supper was not able consistently to suggest the affectional nature of the contact between Jesus and John because of the physical limitations of the table model they employed. Although some very early representations of the Last Supper had the men sitting on the floor at a very low table, artists before and after Leonardo had the thirteen men seated at a round, rectangular, or U-shaped table.[98]

The constraints of such a table and seating model led to picturing John in various postures relative to Jesus: leaning forward, fallen asleep with his head on the table, and with or without Jesus' hand on his head, or having his head encircled by Jesus' arms. The awkwardness of such postures could not have been wholly avoided so long as the artist was not envisioning thirteen men reclining on the floor. Only with that model can the bodily intimacy suggested by the Fourth Gospel be represented in a natural way.

This discussion and the art-historical evidence attest to the ambiguity with which the Fourth Gospel alludes to the special relationship between Jesus and John. My point has been simply that the Johannine account not only allows, but can well be illuminated by the special friendship that should be understood as a natural expression of the normal erotic dimension of Jesus' humanity. No reason or explanation is suggested to account for this friendship, except that John seems to be "the disciple whom Jesus loved more than the others." We should be content to affirm such a reality as we formulate a faith image of Jesus congruent with the apostolic testimony and adequate for our own time.

NOTES

1. Part 1—The Bright Story Begins

2. As will be seen, this redrawing of the picture of Jesus will have immediate implication for revisioning the churches' Christology along the lines indicated toward the end of the previous chapter.

3. This is to employ the criterion of dissimilarity, one of the tests which New Testament scholars use to judge the authenticity or verisimilitude of gospel material. A passage is likely to be historical if, for example, it pictures Jesus in a way that would be uncharacteristic, over-against that of his own cultural situation. C. F. D. Moule has put it this way: ". . . through all the Gospel tradition without exception, there comes a remarkably firmly-drawn portrait of an attractive young man moving freely about among women of all sorts, including the decidedly disreputable, without a trace of

sentimentality, unnaturalness, or prudery, and yet, at every point, maintaining a simple integrity of character. Is this because the environments in which the traditions were preserved and through which they were transmitted were peculiarly favourable to such a portrait? On the contrary, it seems that they were rather hostile to it." C. F. D. Moule, *The Phenomenon of the New Testament* [London: SCM Press, 1967], pp. 53–64.

4. This means, in the language of theological convention, that soteriology precedes Christology.

5. Heschel captured something of this gratuitousness in his language of "radical amazement." Abraham Joshua Heschel, *Man Is Not Alone* [New York: Harper & Row, 1951], pp. 20, 30.

6. The process of ascribing these titles to Jesus was discussed in the preceding chapter.

7. In the fourth century CE the churches opted for "nature" terminology, affirming that both the divine and human "natures" were present in the Christ event: "Therefore, following the holy fathers, we all with one accord teach men to acknowledge one and the same Son, our Lord Jesus Christ, at once complete in Godhead and complete in manhood, truly God and truly man, consisting also of a reasonable soul and body; of one substance [*homoousios*] with the Father as regards his Godhead, and at the same time of one substance with us as regards his manhood; like us in all respects, apart from sin. . . ." [Council of Chalcedon, 451 CE, Act V].

8. The authors sometimes preserved occasional Aramaisms, the presence of which could take us back to the original speech situation of Jesus. His native language was undoubtedly Aramaic, although we should be aware that the Galilee was an ethnically diverse region, that Jesus very likely knew some Greek, and that many aspects of first century CE Palestinian Jewish life give evidence of being considerably Hellenized.

9. E.g., Jesus' harsh words to and about the Pharisees in Matthew 23:1–36.

10. Most contemporary voices who speak of a "black Christ," for example, seem to be aware that this is more metaphorical than descriptive language, designed not to suggest anything abut Jesus' ethnicity, but to point to his solidarity with the oppressed and marginalized persons, as African Americans have often experienced themselves to be in American society. A different dynamic was obviously at work in the Aryanization of Christ which the "German Christian" movement promoted.

11. "Message Christology" is a term suggested by Daphne Hampson, *Theology and Feminism* [Oxford: Blackwell, 1990], p. 62.

12. See, e.g., Edward Schillebeeckx, *Jesus: An Experiment in Christology* [New York: Random House, 1979]; also James H. Charlesworth, ed., *Jesus' Jewishness: Exploring the Place of Jesus in Early Judaism* [New York: Crossroad, 1991].

13. Albeit, to be sure, in their Greek translation, the Septuagint, and arranged in the Septuagint's order.

14. From the "Quicunque Vult" commonly called "The Creed of Saint Athanasius."

15. "Docetism" [from the Greek *doceo*, "to appear"] was a way of speaking about the Christ event which so emphasized the divinity present that the humanity was only apparent.

16. Beverly Wildung Harrison, *Making the Connections: Essays in Feminist Social Ethics* [Boston: Beacon Press, 1985], p. 149.

17. Tom Driver, "Sexuality and Jesus," *Union Seminary Quarterly Review*, Vol. 20 [1965], p. 239. This point is regularly made by contemporary theologians. The following remark is typical: ". . . the full humanity of Christ . . . if it is undermined in any way, Christ is made an alien being and can no longer have any major significance for the human race." [John Macquarrie, *op. cit*, p. 203]. Macquarrie provides an excellent treatment of the rise of classical Christology and attempts at reconstruction. The refrain of his work is the "unambiguous recognition of the complete humanity of Christ." [p. 359] He warns against anything that would be destructive of Christ's humanity. Yet in calling attention to Jesus' necessary sexuality, he does not emphasize the significance of Jesus' maleness, presumably out of a concern to maintain that the humanity of both males and females is equally full humanity. "Sexuality is an essential constitutive element in every human being; and Jesus was a man in the secondary sense that he was of the male sex. But I do not think that any theological importance attaches to this. Being human was essential to Jesus as the Christ, being male was, as far as I can see, contingent." [pp. 359–360]

18. See, e.g., the reference to "the tradition's lack of historical concern." Gunther Bornkamm, *Jesus of Nazareth* [New York: Harper and Row, 1975], p. 19.

19. William E. Phipps, *Was Jesus Married?* [New York: Harper and Row, 1970], p. 36.

20. Phipps, p. 48. Geza Vermes has made a similar observation: "There is complete silence in the Gospels concerning the marital status of Jesus. No wife accompanies him in his public career, or, for that matter, stays at home, as the wives of his followers were expected to do. Such a state of affairs is sufficiently unusual in ancient Jewry to prompt further enquiry." *Jesus the Jew* [New York: Macmillan, 1973], p. 99. Vermes suggests, however, that there was some first century rabbinic opinion that prophecy and marriage were incompatible. That information should make us a bit cautious in assuming that the life of the historical Jesus was indistinguishable from ordinary Jewish life in Palestine.

21. John P. Meier has assessed the evidence with respect to the possibility of Jesus having been married. His own conclusion is that Jesus was not married, and, further, that he was vocationally celibate. John P. Meier, *A Marginal Jew: Rethinking the Historical Jesus* [New York: Doubleday, 1991], pp. 332–345. Commenting on Meier's book, David L. Bartlett has wondered whether some of Meier's judgments might not derive from a reading of the available evidence through the lens of ecclesiastical doctrine. "The Historical Jesus and the Life of Faith," *The Christian Century*, Vol. 109, May 6, 1992, pp. 489–493.

22. Phipps, pp. 66–69.

23. Ascetic, docetic, and Gnostic as well.

24. Rosemary Radford Ruether, "What Do the Synoptics Say About the Sexuality of Jesus?", *Christianity and Crisis*, May 29, 1978. In this chapter I follow out certain clues suggested in Ruether's provocative essay.

25. D. H. Lawrence, *The Man Who Died* [New York: Alfred A. Knopf, 1928].

26. Nikos Kazantzakis, *The Last Temptation of Christ* [New York: Simon and Schuster, 1960].

27. Driver, p. 246.

28. The Johannine author has the sisters report to Jesus about Lazarus' sickness, "He whom you love is ill." [John 11:3]; identifies the situation by saying that "Jesus loved Martha and her sister [Mary] and Lazarus." [John 11:5]; and notes that upon seeing Jesus weep at Lazarus' death, the Jews said, "See, how he loved him." [John 11:36].

29. "The disciple whom Jesus loved" is referred to this way five times [John 13:23; 19:26; 20:2; 21:7; 21:20]. This person [presumably a man] is anonymous, unidentified in the gospel text. The question of his identity and its importance will be discussed in Section 3 of this chapter. Suffice it here to say that I regard the identification of "the Beloved Disciple" with John, the Son of Zebedee, as most probable.

30. Most commentators on the Fourth Gospel no longer attach special significance to the different use of these two verbs meaning "to love." In the report of the sisters and the mourners John uses forms of *phileo*. When describing Jesus' love for the family, he uses a form of *agapao*; Jesus' love for John is named with *agapao* in all cases but one [John 21:2]. I am inclined to agree that the difference in verb use ought not to be stressed, although one should note that this distinction is rather more important to Wescott and Sanders, who see *agapao* "reserved for the description of a love of a particular quality which it is appropriate to ascribe to Jesus." J. N. Sanders, "'Those Whom Jesus Loved'," *New Testament Studies*, Vol. 1, 1954–55, p. 3.

31. See Elisabeth Schuessler-Fiorenza, *In Memory of Her: A Feminist Theological Reconstruction of Christian Origins* [New York: Crossroad Publishing Company, 1984], especially "Women as Paradigms of True Discipleship," pp. 315–334.

32. Leonard Swidler, *Biblical Affirmations of Women* [Philadelphia: Westminster Press, 1979], p. 164. See especially "Positive Elements in the Christian Tradition," pp. 161–325.

33. Michael Grant, *Jesus: An Historian's Review of the Gospels* [New York: Charles Scribner's Sons, 1979], pp. 85–86.

34. Hampson, p. 90.

35. Moule is here referring to Jesus' attitude towards prostitutes in particular.

36. Moule, p. 65. Most scholars agree with Moule that this is "tradition surviving against opposition." p. 61.

37. Over against the formulaic tradition which Paul reports in I Corinthians 15:3–8.

38. John E. Alsup, *The Post-Resurrection Appearance Stories of the Gospel Tradition* [Stuttgart: Calwer Verlag, 1975], p. 268.

39. The non-canonical traditions about Mary have become a subject of much interest by virtue of their use by Dan Brown in his *The DaVinci Code* [New York: Doubleday, 2003]. The texts of the Magdalene tradition are collected in Marvin Meyer and Esther A. DeBoer, eds., *The Gospels of Mary [The Secret Traditions of Mary Magdalene, the Companion of Jesus]*, [San Francisco: HarperSanFrancisco, 2004].

40. *The Gospel of Philip*, 59: 7–10. Tr. Wesley W. Isenberg, in *The Nag Hammadi Library* [San Francisco: Harper and Row, 1977], pp. 135–136.

41. *The Gospel of Philip* 63: 33–35. Tr. Isenberg, p. 138.

42. *The Gospel of Mary* 18: 13–14. Tr. George W. MacRae and R. McL. Wilson, ed. Douglas M Parrott, *The Nag Hammadi Library*, p. 472.

43. *The Gospel of Mary* 18:13–14.

44. Hans-Martin Schenke, "The Function and Background of the Beloved Disciple in the Gospel of John," in Charles W. Hedrick and Robert Hodgson, Jr., *Nag Hammadi, Gnosticism, and Early Christianity* [Peabody, MA: Hendrickson Publishers, 1986], pp. 121–122.

45. Grant, p. 83.

46. Phipps, *Was Jesus Married?*, p. 66.

47. Reginald H. Fuller, *The Formation of the Resurrection Narratives* [New York: Macmillan, 1971], p. 134. See also Willi Marxsen, *The Resurrection of Jesus of Nazareth* [Philadelphia: Fortress Press, 1970], pp. 55–61; and Rudolf Bultmann, *The Gospel of John: A Commentary* [Philadelphia: Westminster Press, 1971], pp. 681–189.

48. Such an inquiry depends, of course, on the prior work of source criticism, redaction history, and philological analysis.

49. My judgment is that the Johannine author[s] did not utilize the present texts of any of the Synoptic gospels, but may have drawn on sources and traditions which the Synoptic evangelists also used in different ways.

50. Raymond E. Brown, *The Birth of the Messiah* [Garden City: Image Books, 1979], pp. 122–164, 697–712.

51. New Testament scholars have not reached general agreement on the dating and significance of *The Gospel of Peter*. Although most regard it as a second century CE text, they also recognize that it may be a development of first century traditions. See: Helmut Koester, *Introduction to the New Testament*. Vol. 2: *History and Literature of Early Christianity* [Philadelphia: Fortress Press, 1982]; Ron Cameron, ed., *The Other Gospels: Non-Canonical Gospel Texts* [Philadelphia: Westminster Press, 1982]; Edgar Hennecke, *New Testament Apocrypha*. Edited by Wilhelm Schneemelcher. English translation edited by R. McL. Wilson, Vol. 1: *Gospels and Related Writings* [Philadelphia: Westminster Press, 1963]. John Dominic Crossan suggests that a first century "Cross Gospel" is a source not only of the *Gospel of Peter*, but also a source of the canonical passion narrative. *The Cross that Spoke. The Origins of the Passion Narrative* [San Francisco: Harper and Row, 1988]. John P. Meier, contra Crossan, regards the *Gospel of Peter* as derivative from and dependent on the Synoptic gospels. Meier, op. cit., p. 117.

52. Marsh, p. 219. For a detailed analysis of the "I am" sayings in John and their parallels in occasional Synoptic usage, see Raymond E. Brown, *The Gospel according to John I-XII* [Garden City: Doubleday and Company, 1966], The Anchor Bible, Vol. 29, pp. 533–538; also Bultmann, p. 225–226.

53. Paul D. Duke, *Irony in the Fourth Gospel* [Atlanta: John Knox Press, 1985], pp. 100–107.

54. See Bultmann, p. 404, following Dibelius. Cp. Thomas' declaration, "My Lord and my God." [John 20:26]. Thus Martha functions in the Fourth Gospel in a way that is similar to Peter's function in the *Gospel according to Matthew* [Matthew 16:16]. See Elisabeth Schuessler-Fiorenza, *In Memory of Her*, p. 329.

55. It is noteworthy that in John 11, the primary role is given to Martha, while in Luke 10:38–42, the "better part" is played by her sister Mary.

56. Paul employs an early Christian hymn in his Philippian Letter: ". . . and every tongue should confess that Jesus Christ is Lord." [Philippians 2:11]

57. It is important to be reminded again that although all of the gospels are theological, and none of them is intentionally biographical in the modern sense, all do, nonetheless, contain genuine historical material, John no less than the Synoptics.

58. A. M. Hunter, *The Gospel According to John* [New York: Cambridge University Press, 1965], p. 184.

59. Xavier Leon-Dufour has called attention to this threefold use of the phrase, and notes "Mary laments the impossibility of finding the body of him whom she loved so much." *Resurrection and the Message of Easter*, tr. R. N. Wilson [New York: Holt, Rinehart and Winston, 1974], p. 76.

60. So Bultmann, p. 686.

61. So Reginald Fuller, who observes, "Mary would like to cling to Jesus as a *theios aner* [divine man]—just as he was in his earthly ministry." [Fuller, p. 138]; Hoskyns and Davey, p. 544.

62. Fuller, "Stop clinging to me." p. 136; also Hoskyns and Davey, p. 544; Dodd, "Stop touching me." p. 443.

63. Bultmann suggests that her action is a friendship gesture, but does not explore any of the contra-cultural aspects of such a movement, involving, as it does, an adult Jewish male and an independent woman: Mary moves to embrace Jesus, according to Bultmann, "as a friend would do to a friend who has come back again." [Bultmann, p. 687] This does point to the personal dynamic present, but it does not have enough verisimilitude unless Mary and Jesus had been accustomed to embracing earlier. Thus, Mary's movement needs to be understood in the context of an intimate touching relationship.

64. Later in this section, we will suggest the probable identity of this person to be John, the Son of Zebedee, and will point out the distortion conveyed by an exclusive use of the title "Beloved Disciple." Until that time, we will follow the convention of referring to the man Jesus loved as "the Beloved Disciple."

65. Clement of Alexandria as cited in Eusebius, *Ecclesiastical History*, VI, 14, 7.

66. For an early acknowledgement of this see Benjamin Bacon, *The Fourth Gospel in Research and Debate* [New York: Moffat, Yard and Co., 1910], pp. 300ff.

67. Bultmann, p. 485.

68. A. Kragerud, cited in Franz Mussner, *The Historical Jesus in the Gospel of John* [New York: Herder and Herder, 1967], p. 56.

69. Bacon, p. 301.

70. Hoskyns and Davey, pp. 442–443.

71. W. Grundmann, cited in Mussner, p. 56.

72. Martin Dibelius, cited in Bultmann, p. 484, n. 3.

73. Brown, *The Community of the Beloved Disciple* [New York: Paulist Press, 1979], p. 31. Also, "Discipleship is the primary Christian category for John, and the disciple par excellence is the Disciple whom Jesus loved." [p. 191]. See Mussner, pp. 56–58.

74. Brown, *The Gospel according to John*, Vol. 1, p. 577. This point is given special importance by Theodore W. Jennings, Jr., *The Man Jesus Loved* [New York: Pilgrim Press, 2003].

75. Brown, *The Gospel according to John*, Vol. 1, p. xcv.

76. See Brown, *The Gospel according to John*, Vol. 1, pp. xcii-xcviii.

77. Lazarus is the preferred choice of Sanders, op. cit., and of Floyd D. Filson, "Who Was the Beloved Disciple?" *Journal of Biblical Literature* Vol. 68 [1949], pp. 83–88. Elisabeth Schuessler-Fiorenza [*In Memory of Her*, p. 329] suggests that we should take with special seriousness the naming of Martha as a disciple whom Jesus loved. [John 11:5].

78. C. K. Barrett, *The Gospel according to John* [Philadelphia: Westminster Press, 1978, 2nd. Ed.], p. 446.

79. Bacon, p. 320. That assessment is not always attended to with the kind of seriousness that it warrants. Recognizing that "the Beloved Disciple" is indeed a "title of extreme and exclusive honor," should make it impossible either to ignore or to sentimentalize its relevance for the Jesus story.

80. This was the conclusion of Brown's investigation, although he later changed his mind somewhat, not in favor of another person, but in favor of suspending judgment. Brown, *The Community of the Beloved Disciple*, pp. 31–34.

81. Hunter, p. 13.

82. Brown, Vol. 29, p. 577.

83. Bultmann, p. 673; see also pp. 484ff.

84. Bultmann, p. 484.

85. Elisabeth Schuessler-Fiorenza, *In Memory of Her*, passim.

86. Brown, *The Community of the Beloved Disciple*, passim.

87. Brown, *The Community of the Beloved Disciple*, p. 153. "This means that a church such as my own, the Roman Catholic, with its great stress on authority and structure, has in the Johannine writings an inbuilt conscience against the abuses of authoritarianism. . . . Like one branch of the Johannine community, we Roman Catholics have come to appreciate that Peter's pastoral role is truly intended by the risen Lord, but the presence in our Scriptures of a disciple whom Jesus loved more than he loved Peter is an eloquent commentary on the relative value of the church office. . . . The greatest dignity to be striven for is neither papal, episcopal, nor priestly; the greatest dignity is that of belonging to the community of the beloved disciples of Jesus Christ." [p. 164].

88. Elisabeth Schuessler-Fiorenza, p. 325.

89. Ibid., p. 324.

90. That a "community of friends" is indeed the way the Johannine circle thought of the church is indicated in the closing of III John: "The friends send you their greetings. Greet the friends." [v. 15]

91. Marsh, p. 493.

92. Hunter, p. 137.

93. Marsh, p. 493.

94. Hoskyns, p. 442.

95. Peter's absence and the Beloved Disciple's presence at the crucifixion is a literary affirmation of the superiority of the Beloved Disciple to Peter.

96. Schenke, p. 123. Schenke holds that the Beloved Disciple is a wholly fictional device of the redactor, functioning in a way analogous to the Pastorals' reference to

Paul. Just as the deutero-Pauline author used "Paul" as a device to ground his views in the figure of the authoritative apostle, so the Johannine redactor uses "the Beloved Disciple" to ground the traditions of his community in the "eye witness" testimony of one who was especially close to Jesus. "This kind of deception may find its explanation, and what is more, its justification only within a particular historical situation of conflict. The circumstances, however, do not point to a conflict within the group, but rather to a confrontation with another [Petrine] tradition. . . ." Schenke, p. 119.

97. Dan Brown [*The Da Vinci Code*] surmises that the figure next to Jesus in this representtion is female.

98. David Alan Brown, "Introduction," *Leonardo's 'Last Supper' Precedents and Reflections* [Washington: National Gallery of Art, 1983], np.

Afterword

We have examined four features of the Christian tradition, suggesting something of the way in which a mode of ambiguity attaches to each. Our concern was not simply to describe that ambiguity, but to explain the importance and necessity of regarding it as an irreducible aspect of the tradition. Embracing ambiguity as a given can make faith more honest, criticism or defense of the tradition more properly focused, relationships in a religiously plural world more humane, and the daily lives of women and men less fearful. Appropriate respect for the earthen vessels can allow the treasure of grace its intended power to mend the fractures in our personal and communal life, and heal the alienation from self, the other, and God that diminish for so many their way of being in the world.

The Christian narrative, like the stories of all religious traditions, displays both a bright and dark side. Acknowledging this ambiguity can lessen communal aggrandizement, and heighten our gratitude for the divine effort to work through free and fragile human beings for the increase of justice on earth.

The Bible discloses the remarkably diverse ways in which women and men have discerned over many centuries the meanings which illuminate our historical experience, and have represented their sense of this giftedness in a plethora of pictures, many of which can nourish even a modern imagination. The deliberate and careful employment of historical critical methods in biblical study is a necessary condition for facilitating acceptance of the ambiguity of its narratives, poems, visions, and letters. Only then can the divine voice, which is no more and no less than the subtext of this anthology, address the reader with nourishing, liberating, and empowering effect.

The central figure of the Christian tradition is, of course, Jesus of Nazareth, and the ambiguity involved here is of two kinds, both of which are aspects of his being unambiguously a fully historical, first century CE Palestinian Jewish male. His significance then and now is not self-evident. [1] One kind of ambiguity is revealed in the continuing process of metaphorical ascription by which the Christian evaluator seeks to give expression to his or her experience of rescue and renovation, construing Jesus variously *as* Son of God, the Christ, Son of Man, etc. [2] Another kind of ambiguity is revealed in the continuing process by which the Christian woman or man interprets a faith or perspectival image of Jesus, witnessed to in the New Testament, as an attractive model for contemporary life—one who strives for justice by standing in solidarity with the marginalized, and especially one who shows how an eros modulated in terms of friendship can enhance an accepting style of life for all persons. Toinette Eugene has suggested just how such a faith or perspectival image of Jesus can function in an including and liberating way:

> To those who so fear the body that they have an inordinate anxiety about all sexuality issues, there is the Word made flesh, God's stamp of approval upon the body as a medium of divine love. To those who find threatening a society wherein sex roles are challenged and become more fluid, to those who find strength primarily in masculine force, and physical power and who take refuge in unquestioned ecclesial and household authority, there is One who strangely inverts our understandings of power and who invites us out of the bondage of patriarchy into the new human reality.[1]

But many wish it were not so.[2] The quest for certainty which John Dewey judged to be the great mistake of the philosophical tradition has its religious analogue as well. For many persons the religious life is not possible without an absolute or set of absolutes to guide their life. They consequently invest a text, a creed, a person, or institutional structure with unquestioned and infallible authority. But to regard any finite thing or being as possessed of infinite value or worth is idolatry, even when, or perhaps especially when such a text or creed or person or institutional structure is identified with God's own truth. For those whose religious life is a quest for certainty, the only alternative to a security provided by such heteronomous authority is the fearful insecurity of having to be a source of authority for oneself. Being free from the constraints of external rule, however, does not necessarily mean that the individual is without direction, or that such self-guidance is wholly subjective and arbitrary. In his Philippian correspondence Paul shows how sensitive he was to the inescapable need for personal decision, since the law has no saving value in itself, but reminded his audience that for the person of faith such decision-making need not issue in immobilizing anxiety; there is a divine power ingredient in human life struggling to achieve some human good: ". . . work out your own salvation with fear and trembling; for it is God who is at work in you . . ." [Phil. 2:12] And in an earlier century John Henry Newman gave moving and what to some persons must have seemed extravagant tribute to the vitality of this divine presence:

> [Conscience] is a messenger from [God], who, both in nature and in grace, speaks to us behind a veil, and teaches us and rules us by his representatives. Conscience is the *aboriginal Vicar of Christ*, a prophet in its informations, a monarch in its peremptoriness, a priest in its blessings and anathemas, and, even though the eternal priesthood throughout the Church should cease to be, in it the sacerdotal principle would remain and would have a sway.[3]

NOTES

1. Toinette M. Eugene, "Faithful Responses to Human Sexuality: Issues Facing the Church Today," *The Chicago Theological Seminary Register*, Vol. LXXXI [Spring 1991], No. 2, pp. 3–4.

2. I have elsewhere described the ability to live with plurality and ambiguity as a mark of psychological maturity. "Fundamentalist literalism, accordingly, can be seen as the religious manifestation of childhood dependence on clearly defined external authority. Such an immature phenomenon in adults expresses a nostalgic desire for conceptual simplicity that seems to be something like a pathological form of religiousness." Berry, *Inquiry*, pp. 136–137.

3. John Henry Newman, "Letter to the Duke of Norfolk," cited in Thomas J. Norris, *Newman and His Theological Method* [Leiden: E. J. Brill, 1977], p. 93. Emphasis mine.

Bibliography

Alsup, John E., *The Post-Resurrection Appearance Stories of the Gospel Tradition* [Stuttgart: Calwer Verlag, 1975].

Asch, Sholem, *The Apostle*, tr. Maurice Samuel [New York: G. P. Putnam's Sons, 1943].

Averill, Lloyd J., "Bishop Spong's 'Rescue' of the Bible, *The Christian Century*, Vol. 108, No. 17, pp. 559–561.

Bacon, Benjamin. *The Fourth Gospel in Research and Debate* [New York: Moffat, Yard and Co., 1910].

Bartlett, David L., "The Historical Jesus and the Life of Faith," *The Christian Century*, Vol. 109, May 6, 1992, pp. 489–493.

Barrett, C. K., *The Gospel According to John* [Philadelphia: Westminster Press, 1978, 2nd ed.].

Berger, Peter, *A Rumor of Angels* [New York: Doubleday and Co., 1969].

Berry, Donald L., "The Bible as an Earthen Vessel: A Plea for Biblical Honesty," *Encounter*, Vol. 58:4, Autumn 1997, pp. 413–418.

———. "The Category Mistake of Messianic Nationalism," *Arab Studies Quarterly*, Vol. 17, No. 4 [Fall 1995], pp. 109.

———. "Do Christians Read from the Hebrew Scriptures?" unpublished manuscript, nd.

———. *An Inquiry into the Nature and Usefulness of a Perspectival Approach to the Study of Religion* [Lewiston: The Edwin Mellen Press, 1991].

———. "Seeking a Theology of the Finite," *The Christian Century*, Vol. 99, No. 29 [September 29, 1982], pp. 953–956.

The Book of Common Prayer [New York: The Church Hymnal Corporation, 1977].

Bornkamm, Gunther, *Jesus of Nazareth* [New York: Harper and Row, 1960].

Brown, Dan, *The Da Vinci Code* [New York: Doubleday, 2003].

Brown, David Alan. *Leonardo's 'Last Supper' Precedents and Reflections* [Washington: National Gallery of Art, 1983].

Brown, Raymond E., *The Birth of the Messiah* [Garden City: Image Books, 1979].

———. *The Community of the Beloved Disciple* [New York: Paulist Press, 1979].

————. *The Gospel According to John I-XII* [Garden City: Doubleday and Company, 1966]

Bultmann, Rudolf, *The Gospel of John: A Commentary* [Philadelphia: Westminster Press, 1971].

————. *Jesus Christ and Mythology* [New York: Charles Scribner's Sons, 1958].

Cameron, Ron, ed., *The Other Gospels: Non-Canonical Gospel Texts* [Philadelphia: Westminster Press, 1982].

Carr, David McLain, *From D to Q: A Study of Early Jewish Interpretations of Solomon's Dream at Gibeon* [Missoula: Scholars Press, 1991].

Charlesworth, James H., ed., *Jesus' Jewishness: Exploring the Place of Jesus in Early Judaism* [New York: Crossroad, 1991].

Crossan, John Dominic, *The Cross That Spoke: The Origins of the Passion Narrative* [San Francisco: Harper and Row, 1988].

————. *The Historical Jesus: The Life of a Mediterranean Jewish Peasant* [San Francisco: Harper and Collins, 1992].

Driver, Tom D., *Patterns of Grace: Human Experience as Word of God* [San Francisco: Harper and Row, 1977].

————. "Sexuality and Jesus," *Union Seminary Quarterly Review*, Vol. 20 [1965], pp. 235–246.

Duke, Paul D., *Irony in the Fourth Gospel* [Atlanta: John Knox Press, 1985].

Eugene, Toinette M., "Faithful Responses to Human Sexuality: Issues Facing the Church Today," *The Chicago Theological Seminary Register*, Vol. LXXXI [Spring 1991], No. 2, pp. 3–4.

Filson, Floyd V., "Who Was the Beloved Disciple?" *Journal of Biblical Literature*, Vol. 68 [1949], pp. 83–88.

————. "Introduction and Exegesis of The Second Epistle to the Corinthians" [New York: Abingdon-Cokesbury Press, 1953], *The Interpreter's Bible*, Vol. 10, pp. 75–77.

Fosdick, Harry Emerson, *The Modern Use of the Bible* [New York: Macmillan Company, 1924].

Fuller, Reginald H., *The Formation of the Resurrection Narratives* [New York: Macmillan, 1971].

Furnish, Victor Paul, *II Corinthians* [Garden City: Doubleday and Co., 1984]. *The Anchor Bible, Vol. 32A*.

Gilkey, Langdon, *Naming the Whirlwind* [Indianapolis: Bobbs-Merrill, 1969].

Grant, Michael, *Jesus: An Historian's Review of the Gospels* [New York: Charles Scribner's Sons, 1979].

————. *Saint Paul* [London: Weidenfeld and Nicolson, 1976].

Gresser, Moshe, "The Old Testament vs. the Tanakh," unpublished manuscript, nd.

Groh, Dennis E., and Jewett, Robert, eds., *The Living Text: Essays in Honor of Ernest W. Saunders* [Lanham: University Press of America, 1985].

Hampson, Daphne, *Theology and Feminism* [Oxford: Blackwell, 1900].

Harrison, Beverly Wildung, *Making the Connections: Essays in Feminist Social Ethics* [Boston: Beacon Press, 1985].

Hennecke, Edgar, *New Testament Apocrypha* [Philadelphia: Westminster Press, 1963, 1963].

Heschel, Abraham Joshua, *Man Is Not Alone* [New York: Harper & Row, 1951].

Holmberg, Bengt, *Paul and Power* [Philadelphia: Fortress Press, 1978].

Hoskyns, Edwin, *The Fourth Gospel*, F. N. Davey, ed. [London: Faber and Faber, 1947].

Hunter, A. M., *The Gospel According to John* [New York: Cambridge University Press, 1965].

Jennings, Jr., Theodore W., *The Man Jesus Loved* [New York: Pilgrim Press, 2003].

Jones, Alexander, gen. ed., *The Jerusalem Bible* [Garden City: Doubleday and Co., 1966].

Kaufman, Gordon D., *The Theological Imagination: Constructing the Concept of God* [Philadelphia: Westminster Press, 1981].

Kazantzakis, Nikos, *The Last Temptation of Christ* [New York: Simon and Schuster, 1960].

Koester, Helmut, *Introduction to the New Testament*, Vol. 2: *History and Literature of Early Christianity* [Philadelphia: Fortress Press, 1982].

Lawrence, D. H., *The Man Who Died* [New York: Simon and Schuster, 1960].

Leon-Dufour, Xavier, *Resurrection and the Message of Easter*, tr. R. N. Wilson [New York: Holt, Rinehart and Winston, 1974].

Macquarrie, John, *Jesus Christ in Contemporary Thought* [Philadelphia: Trinity Press International, 1900].

Mann, C. S., *Mark* [Garden City: Doubleday and Co., 1986], *The Anchor Bible* Vol. 27.

Marxsen, Willi, *The Resurrection of Jesus of Nazareth* [Philadelphia; Fortress Press, 1970].

McFague, Sallie, *Metaphorical Theology* [Philadelphia: Fortress Press, 1982].

———. *Models of God* [Philadelphia: Fortress Press, 1987].

Meeks, Wayne A., gen. ed., *The HarperCollins Study Bible [NRSV]* [New York: HarperCollins, 1993].

———. *The Writings of St. Paul* [New York: W. W. Norton and Co., 1972].

Meier, John P., *A Marginal Jew: Rethinking the Historical Jesus* [New York: Doubleday, 1991].

Metzger, Bruce M., *The Text of the New Testament: Its Transmission, Corruption, and Restoration* [New York and Oxford: Oxford University Press, 1992].

———, and Murphy, Roland, eds. *The New Oxford Annotated Bible with the Apocryphal/Deuterocanonical Books. NRSV* [New York: Oxford University Press, 1991].

Meyer, Marvin and De Boer, Esther A., eds., *The Gospels of Mary [The Secret Tradition of Mary Magdalene, The Companion of Jesus]* [San Francisco: HarperSanFrancisco, 2004].

Moule, C. F. D., *The Phenomenon of the New Testament* [London: SCM Press, 1967].

Murphy, Roland, "Old Testament/Tanakh—Canon and Interpretation," in Roger Brooks and John J. Collins, ed., *Hebrew Bible or Old Testament?* [Notre Dame: University of Notre Dame Press, 1990].

Mussner, Franz, *The Historical Jesus in the Gospel of John* [New York: Herder and Herder, 1967].

Nall, Stephen F., *The Advocate*, Vol. 4, No. 1 [April 1991].

Nelson, Ted, *The Advocate*, Vol. 4, No. 1 [April 1991].

Newman, John Henry, *An Essay on the Development of Christian Doctrine*, ed. J. M. Cameron [Baltimore: Penguin Books, 1974].

——. *Tracts for the Times* Vol. VI, No. 85 [London: J. G. F. and J. Rivington and J. H. Parker, 1840].

Nock, Arthur Darby, *St. Paul* [New York: Harper and Brothers, 1937].

Norris, Thomas J., *Newman and His Theological Method* [Leiden: E. J. Brill, 1977].

Phipps, William E., *Was Jesus Married?* [New York: Harper and Row, 1970].

Robinson, John A. T., *Honest to God* [Philadelphia: Westminster Press, 1963].

Ruether, Rosemary Radford, "What Do the Synoptics Say About the Sexuality of Jesus?" *Christianity and Crisis*, May 29, 1978.

Sanders, J. N., "'Those Whom Jesus Loved'," *New Testament Studies*, Vol. 1, 1954–55.

Schenke, Hans-Martin, "The Function and Background of the Beloved Disciple in the Gospel of John," in Charles W. Hedrick and Robert Hodgson, Jr., *Nag Hammadi, Gnosticism, and Early Christianity* [Peabody, MA: Hendrickson Publishers, 1986], pp. 121–122.

Schillebeeckx, Edward, *Jesus: An Experiment in Christology* [New York: Random House, 1979].

Schuessler-Fiorenza, Elisabeth, *But She Said* [Boston: Beacon Press, 1992].

——. *Jesus: Miriam's Child, Sophia's Prophet* [New York: Continuum, 1994].

——. *In Memory of Her: A Feminist Theological Reconstruction of Christian Origins* [New York: Crossroad Publishing Company, 1984].

Selby, Donald Joseph, *Toward an Understanding of St. Paul* [Englewood Cliffs: Prentice-Hall, 1962].

Spong, John, *Living in Sin: A Bishop Rethinks Human Sexuality* [San Francisco: Harper & Row, 1988].

——. *Rescuing the Bible from Fundamentalism* [San Francisco: Harper and Row, 1991.

Swidler, Leonard, *Biblical Affirmations of Women* [Philadelphia: Westminster Press, 1979].

Vermes, Geza, *Jesus the Jew* [New York: Macmillan, 1973].

Wilder, Amos Niven, *Theopoetic* [Philadelphia: Fortress Press, 1976].

Winkler, John J., "Unnatural Acts: Erotic Protocols in Artemidoros' *Dream Analysis*, in *The Constraints of Desire* [New York and London: Routledge, 1990], pp. 17–44.

Witherington, Ben, "The Anti-Feminist Tendencies of the 'Western' Text in Acts," *Journal of Biblical Literature*, Vol. 103 [1984], 82–84.

Also by Donald L. Berry

Mutuality: The Vision of Martin Buber [Albany: State University
of New York Press, 1985]

Traveler's Advisory [Lewiston: The Edwin Mellen Press, 1990]
[Mellen Poetry Series Volume 9]

*An Inquiry into the Nature and Usefulness Of a Perspectival Approach to
the Study of Religion* [Lewiston: The Edwin Mellen Press, 1991]